E

With Intention is for the everyday hero. If something is getting you down, in your way, or causing you pain, this book will show you the way forward. With Jon Giganti as your guide, your journey begins as soon as you crack open this gem of a book.

—Michael Port
New York Times and *Wall Street Journal*
Bestselling Author of *Steal the Show*

Jon's vulnerability is both refreshing and needed in today's world. He provides a practical and executable framework to lead your life with greater intention and ownership. This book will help you become the person you were called to be and empower you to realize that past failures don't define you. The principles Jon shares will enable you to evolve, serve others, and work toward your full potential. It is an absolute must-read.

—Alan Stein, Jr.
Keynote Speaker, Corporate Performance Coach,
and Author of *Raise Your Game*

Jon has spent years learning, studying, and applying what the best of the best do. Elite performers and leaders have a growth mentality and always focus on serving others. When you combine the two, great things can happen. Reading this book will get you closer to your potential as a performer and a leader.

—Caleb Porter
Two-time Major League Soccer Championship Head Coach - Portland Timbers (2015), Columbus Crew (2020)

Jon spoke to my team a few years ago, sharing the principles of living with intention. We were blown away by his passion and ability to help us identify and take action to change our professional and personal lives for the better. I'm still using several of the ideas today and seeing real results. Now, a few years later, Jon has continued to grow and is sharing even more of his learnings. If you're looking for a real-world guide with easy application to take ownership and create a new future, this is the book for you.

—Josh Thompson
Senior Vice President, GM Onstar Insurance

I'm sure if asked, "Do you want to grow?", you'd answer yes. Most of us do. The challenge is we have not *systematized* an approach to our growth; we've not identified the principles to practice. In his wonderful book, Jon uses his own story and the lessons extracted, along with science and real-world examples to support your growth and to lay the foundation of principles you'll likely weave into your approach to creating a life of resilience and fulfillment. Because after all, that's what you're here for. Peace.

—Danny Bader
Bestselling Author of *Back to Life*: *The Path of Resilience*

Jon's storytelling reels me in. I'm there with him, see myself in him. I see and feel seen. The wisdom he gathered and wrapped into a simple, but not simplistic, framework is inspiring, actionable, and must-have knowledge for aspiring leaders in business and life.

—Mike Williams
Co-CEO *Doing to Done*, Author of *Doing to Done*,
Co-author of *Getting Things Done for Teens*

I have known Jon for over a decade and with each interaction I am always left energized and empowered. With Intention has captured this same essence through Jon's willingness to share the trials of his personal journey. When I got a copy of With Intention I couldn't put it down. His stories are so relatable that this is one of those books that feels that it was written directly to the reader, and his systemized approach makes With Intention a must read.

—Eric Nichols
Head Men's Soccer Coach,
Bowling Green State University

With Intention is Jon's way of living his mission; helping others (period). This work is a wakeup call to "pay *intention*" and don't waste any more time. Jon literally applies a method that everyone can step through to know *how* to overcome and move forward. I've had a front row seat to witness Jon apply what he is sharing in this book to his life."

—Chris Shepherd
Husband, Father of 3 boys, Bible Study Leader &
Speaker, Vice President, Center of Excellence - CCC
Intelligent Solutions

Jon has created a simplified approach that can be used in all facets of life. If you're a kid heading off to college or an executive of a major company, these five components will resonate and allow a deep dive into one's self, personally or professionally. Jon's life experiences are experiences many have faced, but unlike so many, he was able to identify, focus and create a solution that worked for him and will work for others. This is a must read for anyone who is in pursuit of more.

—Scott Christy
Vice President of Sales - Copart

WITH INTENTION

WITH INTENTION

A Proven Path to Uncommon Results,
Unleashed Influence, and Ultimate Fulfillment

JON GIGANTI

ethos
collective

Published by Ethos Collective™ PO Box 43, Powell, OH 43065
www.EthosCollective.vip

Identifiers:
LCCN: 2022917577
ISBN: 978-1-63680-104-9 (paperback)
ISBN: 978-1-63680-105-6 (hardback)
ISBN: 978-1-63680-106-3 (ebook)

Available in paperback, hardback, e-book, and audiobook

Discover Your With Intention Quotient™ (WIQ)

Take the Free Assessment

https://training.jongiganti.com/assessment

For Michelle, Gabe, Reese & Emerson - You fuel me and inspire me to live with intention everyday. I love you to the moon and back!

CONTENTS

Foreword xv
Note to the Reader xvii
Introduction xxi

Part 1: The Problem

Chapter 1: Lack of Growing Intentionally (I Don't) 3

Lack of Self-Awareness (I don't know.) 9
Lack of Ownership (I don't care.) 14
Lack of Vision (I don't see.) 17
Lack of Discipline (I don't try.) 19
Lack of Growth (I don't improve.) 22

Chapter 2: Lack of Serving Intentionally (I Can't) 26

Lack of Authenticity (I can't be honest.) 28
Lack of Compassion (I can't empathize.) 30
Lack of Creativity (I can't produce.) 33
Lack of Humility (I can't let go.) 34
Lack of Energy (I can't keep up.) 36

Chapter 3: Three Outcomes of Intention
                    Deficit (I am Not) 38

Lack of Results (I am not contributing.) 40
Lack of Influence (I am not important.) 41
Lack of Fulfillment (I am not fulfilled.) 42

Part 2: The Path

Chapter 4: Build Yourself (I Do). 47

Awareness (I know.)—Identify your personal blind
spots and professional gaps so you can step into
your genius and make your time count. 49

Agency (I care.)—Take complete ownership of
your past and present so your focus stops
getting "hacked." 55

Ambition (I see.): Create a new future that reflects
your ideal legacy. 60

Action (I try.)—Leverage the right mindset so you
can win more days and achieve your vision. 71

Adjustment (I improve.)—Forever evolve so you
contribute to your world in a meaningful way. . . 86

Chapter 5: Build into Others (I Can) 92

Sincerity (I can be honest.)—Serve others
authentically so you can build trust and rapport. . 94

Empathy (I can empathize.)—Listen with your
heart and help others feel heard. 96

Resourcefulness (I can produce.)—Determine how to
get the job done, even when times are tough. 97

Value (I can provide.)—Deliver value in every
interaction so you will be relied upon. 100

Energy (I can keep up.)—Bring positive energy
to your relationships and interactions. 101

Part 3: The Pinnacle

Chapter 6: The Outcomes of With Intention (I Am). . . 109

Results (I am contributing.) 111

Influence (I am important.) 113

Fulfillment (I am joyful.) 114

Afterword 115
Appendix: Additional List of Standards from My Core . . 117
Acknowledgments 123
Notes. 129
About the Author. 131

FOREWORD

Attitudes are infectious. Spend time with a negative person—someone living without intention— and you'll soon become a mess. Spend time with a positive person—someone living with intention—and you'll soon become a masterpiece.

Jon Giganti is the latter, a giver and an outlier.

I've known Jon for nearly a decade and I've been impressed. I've invited him to my stage, and he's spoken to my clients. Everyone leaves better— thinking clearer and living deeper. Jon has this effect on people.

He has flaws—we all do. His might be overthinking the future and underestimating his genius. But he does what he says and he lives with intention. Who does that?

When it came time to read his book, I knew it would be good. But when I read the final version, I was truly pleased.

This is his moment.

Jon is a student of success and a practitioner of personal growth. He synthesized the greats and he added to the conversation. I got caught up in his stories and mesmerized by his memories.

I know he's onto something bigger than himself. *Intention deficit disorder*? Now that's worth pondering. Read the back cover copy again. It's deep and relevant and agitating.

That's the trouble with truth. It sets us free, but it also hurts.

Jon serves up some raw truth in this book. Most people describe his style as refreshingly honest. He walks with authenticity, and for this reason, people love or loathe him.

Not everyone is ready for truth. Some will camp out in the shadows because they think it's safer. But Jon will demonstrate that there's freedom in the light. This is where we experience healing and grace.

Jon is the product of both. And because he has received, he now has something to give. You—the reader—will feel this immediately.

His subtitle says it all: *A Proven Path to Uncommon Results, Unleashed Influence, and Ultimate Fulfillment.*

If you're ready for uncommon results, well then, buckle up. Jon is your tour guide to transformation. He'll show you the path. But only you can walk it.

Jon has always been a friend. Now it's exciting to now sit under his teaching. I couldn't be more proud. He's a soul on fire and he's igniting others.

Get ready to live with even more intention.

Well done, Jon. Now it's up to us—each one of us. You've convinced us that now is our time too.

—Kary Oberbrunner, CEO Igniting Souls, and
Wall Street Journal and *USA Today* Bestselling Author

NOTE TO THE READER

The book you're about to read reveals a secret. My secret. It's one that nearly destroyed my marriage, my career, and my legacy as a father. Because of my silence, my mental health suffered. My relationship with God—or lack thereof—also suffered. I failed to see the needs of the people around me because I was caught up inside an internal prison.

I suffered from a disease called *intention deficit disorder*.

You've probably never heard of it. At the time of this writing, you won't find it in a medical book either. And yet very soon, you might realize you also suffer from it.

* * *

You're a work in progress. I am too.

The world tells us we should be perfect and have everything figured out. The truth is—it's okay if you're struggling. Perfection is a terrible master and an even worse goal.

Have you heard of the Hero's Journey? It's the framework for most Hollywood movies. A guy by the name of Joseph Campbell created it. George Lucas made it famous because he wrote *Star Wars* with the Hero's Journey in mind.

It's this: A character is on a journey. They get "punched in the face." A guide comes along to help. They make their way back and return with the magic elixir or the holy grail and save the day.

Many stories follow this path.

Jesus dies on a Friday and rises on a Sunday.

Nelson Mandela goes to jail for twenty-seven years for a crime he didn't commit, never holds a grudge, then gets out of prison and becomes the first black president of South Africa.

Here's the thing—you don't have to be someone famous to embrace the Hero's Journey. It's yours for the taking every day.

And it's the biggest mindset shift you can leverage in your life.

And if you didn't know, adversity is coming for you, and you will bounce back. I know—not always easy to do. There's something about a victim mindset that's comfortable. There aren't expectations when you're a victim. You can complain and blame and gossip and throw people under the bus.

Or you can pick yourself up, dust yourself off, and figure out how to advance. How to rebuild. How to keep going.

It is your journey and your story. You have the power to change it. You have the power to move forward—to advance.

I want you to be the hero in your journey so you can become the guide in someone else's.

That's the key here—you pay it forward. You learn from your journey and teach others.

You have the power to be more intentional in your life. I also believe it's not as hard as you might think it is.

Here's what I mean. Have you ever looked in the mirror and wondered why you weren't further ahead?

(Long pause . . .)

I have. I've been there. And it's a bad place to be. We're going to change that. From now on, you will become better—day by day.

This isn't about perfection. It's about imperfect progress.

With Intention is a path—a path that works. I've leveraged it in my own life and other people have leveraged it to find freedom in their own lives.

It's not rocket science. As a matter of fact, it's simple. It's supposed to be that way. Simple to understand, difficult to do.

But you're not alone. I'm honored to be your guide on this journey as you read these pages. Let me start by encouraging you in case no one has ever said these words to you:

I believe in you.

And if you're wondering if you're ready, the answer is no. No one is ever fully ready to begin the journey to living with intention.

I wasn't. None of us are.

The key is to start, and the key is to keep going—one step at a time.

I'll be here with you.

—Jon

INTRODUCTION

Failure to Pay Intention

Damaged people are dangerous.
They know they can survive.
—Josephine Hart

I hung up the phone and thought my career was over.

That was the day I realized I sucked at my job.

I had been removed from my top account three months earlier, and now I'd received a phone call from my second biggest account, and it wasn't good news.

This client was a good friend.

Just six months earlier, I had spent the weekend hanging out with his family in San Antonio. We had a glorious day together. We spent the afternoon at his son's football game where his daughter was also cheerleading. The warm Texas sun combined with the pride of hanging out with one of my top clients and friends . . . I felt unstoppable.

Cocksure and arrogant.

I thought I was "the man"—whatever that means.

The day before that weekend in sunny Texas, I stopped at the mall to purchase some Dallas Cowboys gear. Gifts were my thing. I could build a relationship with anyone. That part was easy. My clients became fast friends, but as you'll learn in this book, business isn't only about friendship. It may get you started, but business must be about value. Trust and value. One without the other doesn't work.

After the football game and gift-giving, we watched a boxing match at my client's house. His father-in-law made the best pork rinds I've ever tasted. I don't even like pork rinds, but that day I did. His whole family came over, and I was the out-of-town friend who got to meet everyone.

Felt a little like a celebrity, even.

The last shot of Patron went down after the boxing match ended. I got a ride back to my hotel and flew home to Ohio the next day.

I felt he was more than a client.

That's what made this phone call so hard.

That day, I was driving in the Short North neighborhood—an artsy corner—in Columbus, Ohio. I was on a narrow side street off the main road. My phone rang. I looked down and then hit the green button. "Hey, Socio!" (This is what we called each other. *Socio* is a term of endearment in the Hispanic culture and means "friend.")

I knew right away something was off—maybe something different in his voice.

After some small talk, he simply said to me, "Jon, we're moving the business."

Crap! I knew I was in trouble.

This was my second "difficult" phone call in three months. The first one was from my boss. He'd called and told me he was taking me off my biggest account. That meant most of the business I managed was going away—never good for a sales rep.

My career was on life support.

*   *   *

How did I get here? How do any of us "get here?"

Looking back now, it's so clear. I failed to pay intention.

You might think that last word was an accident. *He means to pay "attention," right?*

Nope. I mean I failed to pay intention. (Take that, spell check that's still telling me I typed it incorrectly.)

Let me explain.

Our world has a problem . . . a *big* problem.

And no one seems to be talking about it—at least until now.

PART 1
THE PROBLEM
Intention Deficit Disorder

CHAPTER 1

LACK OF GROWING INTENTIONALLY (I DON'T)

Growth happens by intention—not by accident.

We are all a little broken, but last time I
checked, broken crayons still color the same.
—Trent Shelton

W e want the prize without the pain. We dream of
the crown without the cross. But deep in our gut,
we all know this isn't the path toward greatness.
It's wishful thinking, and that's all it is.

"Everyone wants to go to heaven, but nobody wants to die." Joe Louis captured the crux of human desire. His words aren't pretty, but they're true, and so is this book.

We'll travel down the gritty path together, but first a glimpse of the glory on the other side. Holding this back won't serve you or your story. Quite the opposite. Unless you see where we're headed, when things get tough, you may be tempted to pack it in early.

That would be a shame because we're all connected. When you win, we all win. But when you give up, a little piece of us dies as well.

Therefore, here's a peek at the prize, the reward that awaits you: Sincerity. Empathy. Resourcefulness. Value. Energy.

With Intention Wheel—Others

What do you think?

I didn't say sex, fame, money, power, and ego.

Why not?

Because those wouldn't satisfy your soul—not really. Look no further than the headlines, newsfeeds, or trending topics. These shallow substitutes won't fill you. This is why some of the most famous celebrities take their lives. They're not fulfilled. They wonder, *Is this all there is?*

No. It's not.

Try these on for size instead.

Sincerity. Empathy. Resourcefulness. Value. Energy.

Notice the word they spell: SERVE. This is intentional.

Maybe you're thinking, *That's great—but how do I get it, if I even* want *it?*

Glad you asked. I call it the With Intention Wheel. And it's only appropriated through five steps: Awareness. Agency. Ambition. Action. Adjustment.

There's no shortcut, no pill, no upgrade. It's gained through grit and embodied through effort.

Simple? Yes!

But it requires a death. Nobody arrives with intention unless some part of them dies.

Sounds fun, hey?

Like I said, "Everyone wants to go to heaven, but nobody wants to die."

I certainly didn't. Then again, I didn't have an option unless I wanted my job, my family, and my sanity to end.

Maybe you know how I felt?

Maybe you don't have an option either?

*   *   *

Someone close to me deals with ADHD (attention deficit hyperactivity disorder). Because of this, it can be a challenge for them to navigate school, sports, and basic tasks at home. The struggle to focus and self-regulate is a significant obstacle.

Dr. Russell Barkley is a world-renowned psychologist who specializes in ADHD. I had the chance to sit down and interview him for my podcast. As I was preparing for the interview, I read one of his books and kept thinking about how little we know about how our brains work. I was interested in learning more.

I was thinking about the concept of intention when I read his work. It just so happened that I was also researching information about ADHD. As I was preparing for our conversation, I came across a YouTube video of Dr. Barkley talking about IDD— intention deficit disorder. He was giving a lecture and made the case that attention deficit is a lack of intention as opposed to a lack of attention. In other words, a person doesn't do what they intended to do.

It's not a knowledge problem. Rather, it's a doing problem. We don't do what we know we need to do.

Intention deficit disorder is the gap between knowing and doing.

Here's a snippet of what Dr. Barkley said in his lecture.

ADHD creates a near-sightedness to time so
that the person with the disorder cannot organize

to the delayed future but only to the imminent future. And so everything in life becomes a crisis. But the crisis was avoidable, and no one has any patience with this because they see this as a moral failing. "You could've chosen to get ready, but you didn't." It is phrased as a form of laziness . . . but we know it as the executive failure it really is. This disorder precludes you from organizing across time. So you live in the moment, and you cannot organize very large hierarchically sequenced behavior across time. It means that future-directed behavior is intentional behavior, which means ADD is actually IDD: intention deficit disorder. "I don't seem to be able to accomplish most of the things I intended to do." You can call that a short attention span, but I think "intention deficit disorder" captures it much better.[1]

His words pierced me. Finally, someone had put words to the way I felt. He went on to unpack the disorder even further.

The back part of the brain acquires knowledge. The front part of the brain puts it in play. ADHD has separated these two like a meat cleaver, so it really doesn't matter what you know; you can't use it as effectively as other people can. ADHD is a performance disorder. You can't perform the things you know how to do. It is not a knowledge disorder.

Bottom line, someone with ADHD *knows* how to do something, but this same person is unable to *do* that something. Experts call this a performance gap—we're struggling to do what we need to do.

7

Sound familiar?

I know I shouldn't have consumed that ice cream sundae from Dairy Queen late last night, but I still did. If I keep making those choices, then in a short amount of time, I will gain weight.

Maybe intention deficit disorder affects more people than we think.

Maybe we're all dealing with this gap between knowing and doing.

Maybe if we can close this gap, we'll experience uncommon results, unleashed influence, and ultimate fulfillment.

But how?

*   *   *

First, let's dive into the problems that surface when you're *not* living with intention. The figure below will help bring some clarity. I call it the Without Intention Wheel.

Without Intention Wheel—Self

In this mindset, it's easy to live in a reactive state. Distractions are all around us, and survival is the norm.

The problem runs deeper than this with a lot of our challenges occurring below the surface, maybe even in our subconscious. We're getting hacked without even knowing it.

There are five "lacks" that hold us back from growth:

1. Lack of Self-Awareness
2. Lack of Ownership
3. Lack of Vision
4. Lack of Discipline
5. Lack of Growth

The good news is that with some *intentional* effort— pun intended—you can turn these liabilities into assets. I'll take the lead and remove my mask. I'll share how far I fell because I lacked intention. Maybe my near self-destruction will help you experience more success sooner. Let's unpack each component and discover how it's holding you back.

Lack of Self-Awareness (I don't know.)

In Columbus that day, sitting in my Mercedes (perhaps another false sign of success I used to insulate myself from the truth), I was thirty-five years old. Five years prior, my company had promoted me to my dream job—my first big-time sales role.

I wasn't ready.

There were many broken pieces swimming around my soul, manifesting their jagged edges at the most inopportune times and in unpredictable ways.

I remember standing in the guidance counselor's office at age ten. I looked at the floor, ashamed to make eye contact. They'd admitted my dad to the hospital. Nervous breakdown, I guess. At least that's what they told me.

"Jon, I heard about your dad. Just curious to know how you are doing?"

"I'm great . . . I'm good," I said, lying. I think I had straight A's at the time.

That was the end of that conversation. It's the first time I recall sweeping something under the rug. Even with the challenges at home, I was a "privileged kid" by many standards. I had two older brothers, and there's little doubt we had a mom and dad who loved and supported us.

My parents were great, but like all families, we had secrets. My dad's breakdown was one of them. The world teaches us to keep things inside. We're taught to keep pressing forward to the detriment of self-reflection. Curiosity is out. Conformity is in.

We never talked about what happened. I wasn't mature enough, nor did I have the self-awareness to know what I was feeling. Too bad, because as an adult, I now know self-awareness has the potential to create a breakthrough. My friend and bestselling author James Clear says, "The process of behavior change starts with self-awareness."

Back then, I wasn't open to change or self-awareness. Many people aren't. My guess is, like the rest of humanity, you're moving fast. Life isn't slowing down, and time is undefeated. The minutes, days, and months keep clipping by.

We're in a rat race, simply trying to survive. Slowing down is difficult. This is why it's a challenge to dig deep and work on yourself.

Our brains are complex and the lizard brain is partially to blame. According to *Brain Rules* by molecular biologist and brain researcher John Medina, we have three parts of our brains that rule our thoughts, emotions, and actions.

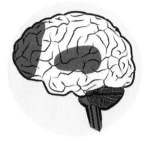

- **Lower Reptilian Brain:** This is the "fight-or-flight" part of your brain. This region is all about acting and reacting. Think impulse. It can serve us well at times, and it can crush us at times. It can leave you frozen in a perceived crisis—the "deer-in-the-headlights" response. Yogis call this the "monkey brain." It's where we have so many thoughts, and we can't turn them off.

- **Middle Mammal Brain:** This is the seat of your emotions—your inner drama king or queen. It's where powerful feelings of love, joy, sadness, anger, grief, jealousy, and pleasure arise. Our thoughts lead to feelings, always.

- **Upper Primate Brain:** The upper or primate brain is like *Star Trek*'s Mr. Spock. It's the part that weighs a situation logically and rationally and generates a conscious plan of action. This neocortex collects data from the reptile and mammal brains, sifts it, analyzes it, and makes practical, smart, and ethical decisions. We can take our lower and middle brains (thoughts and emotions) and make rational decisions based on data.

We have 6,200 unique thoughts per day.[2] In a 24-hour day, that's 258 unique thoughts per hour or about 4 per minute. Although potentially overwhelming, understanding your brain can unlock some powerful components, specifically interference and Resistance.

Interference

Timothy Gallwey wrote a book in the 1970s called *The Inner Game of Tennis*. As a tennis coach, he wanted to figure out a way to teach his students and how to perform more consistently. He noticed many of his students were held back by some kind of mental block. It wasn't that they didn't have the talent or skill to produce. Something was holding them back. He called this "interference."

Gallwey developed a formula: Performance= Potential - Interference.

Here's what it means. We all have potential, but interference gets in the way. The interference is different for everyone, and it doesn't matter what it is. The important thing is to understand your interference.

Even the best athletes, business executives salespeople or doctors experience interference. If you're human, you deal with it. Our brains are wired for interference. This fight or flight response exists to protect us.

The challenge is that too many people lack an understanding or self-awareness because they aren't looking for it. But what if you could consistently perform at an optimal level? Or maybe you are a top performer, but you want to get to the next level. Simply understanding and having this self-awareness could be an important first step.

Interference comes in many forms: that little voice in your head telling you you're not good enough, or fear. Interference can be tangible things like social media addiction or even bad influences in your life (people, mindless TV, etc.). The list goes on and on. For me, it's even something as basic as breathing. I tend to hold my breath at times, and it leads to an increase in anxiety. I do it subconsciously. I've learned to combat this interference by remaining intentional and reminding myself to breathe deeply. When I do that, it always helps.

Resistance

While writing this book, I've experienced what Steven Pressfield calls Resistance. Pressfield has published many nonfiction books, including *The War of Art* and *Turning Pro*. He also wrote *The Legend of Bagger Vance*, a popular Hollywood movie.

Pressfield writes on a common theme: the force holding us back from creative breakthroughs. This Resistance is the real deal. As I'm writing outside in Westerville, Ohio, distractions pop up all around me. People are walking by, a dog just took a sniff of my leg, and my phone just buzzed with a text message notification. Then, there's the voice in my head that's telling me right now may not be the best time to write. This is all Resistance.

Anytime you commit to produce, create, or perform, a force rises to oppose you. Resistance is everywhere. Those 6,200 thoughts will conspire to work against you. They'll kill your creativity and commitment unless you're self-aware. Resistance is inevitable. The true test is how you respond to it. In the second part of this book, together, we'll develop a strategic plan to combat Resistance. For now, simply acknowledge its existence.

Lack of Ownership (I don't care.)

With those two phone calls, the one from my former client firing me and the one from my boss addressing my underperformance, I found myself demoted. My initial reaction was to blame others for it.

I felt sorry for myself.

Let me give you some background on the first call. A key contact at one of my accounts dropped me off at the airport in Hartford, Connecticut. We had just finished some training. I had been trying to get this account to move to our new software platform for many months. No matter what I tried, I simply couldn't get them to transition, and the internal pressure mounted inside my brain.

I told this client they were getting lost in the minutiae of the project and they needed to move. I challenged him with more force than usual, evidenced by my mannerisms and tone. Sure, I was a bit out of character, but I certainly didn't feel any ill will walking into the Hartford airport. I made my way through security and boarded my flight back to Ohio, unaware of the firestorm I had initiated.

A couple of days later, my boss forwarded an email from this client. My heart sank. The word *minutiae* was underlined and bolded at least five times.

This guy didn't like my approach, and I was promptly removed from the account. I was pissed. This guy had overstepped and taken my words out of context.

Within a couple of weeks, I moved to another team. I traveled with my new boss, Ray, to New Orleans. I knew him well and considered him a good friend. I complained about getting a raw deal.

He stopped, looked me straight in the eyes, and called me out. "Jon, where there's smoke there's fire. And you have smoke at multiple accounts. You can complain about it or do something about it."

Message heard, but not yet fully received.

While I'd like to say I took ownership immediately, I didn't. It's easier to blame and complain. It's easier to be the victim.

*　*　*

I took a class a few years back. The guy leading it, Tim Kight, mentioned a concept called BCD. Intrigued, I wondered what he meant. When he explained it further, the truth hit me like a ton of bricks. BCD stands for blame, complain, and defend, and it holds most people back.

What about you? Do you blame, complain, or defend?

I do. It's inside all of us—human nature, you know? Although we can train ourselves to BCD less, eradicating it is near impossible.

Martin Seligman wrote a brilliant book called *Learned Optimism*. This renowned psychologist and researcher reveals how optimism is a choice. We can embody learned optimism or learned helplessness.

When our lizard brain seeks out excuses for things not going our way, in that moment we are choosing to be helpless, to be victims.

Reflect on your own life. Are you someone who's always finding excuses? Blaming others? Complaining? Gossiping? Stirring things up?

If so, don't write yourself off. There's hope for you, I promise. I know because I'm proof.

At times, I lean toward the negative. Like everyone else, I can get caught up in this vicious loop:

Woe is me.

Why did this happen?

The world is out to get me.

The victim mentality shows up anywhere and everywhere in life—relationships, businesses, and politics. How many teams shrug off a loss with the old "It's just not our day"?

I spend a bunch of my time in the corporate world leading a sales team for a SaaS (software as a service) company. We strive to be a high-performing organization. Ownership is one of our core values. Values are great, but it's who you are in moments of truth that matters.

Great companies take ownership for everything— the good and the bad. A few months back, my team lost a deal. Of course, there are many reasons it didn't come through. Our implementation team didn't deliver the product the right way, and it set us back. Our consulting team didn't develop the right ROI, and we set the wrong expectations. Looking back, I can see the deal was not set up for success. In talking to our rep, it's easy to blame the product or the teams but, ultimately, the buck stops with us. It's our job to manage the teams, the rollout, and the expectations with the customer.

We fell short. I own that now.

The temptation was to blame other people or things— to find an excuse. When I was typing up my email to our leadership team to let them know we lost the deal, my first draft dished out the blame. Then I had to pause, look in the mirror, and make sure I took ownership for my part.

This shift makes all the difference and sets the tone for everything else.

We'll do a post-mortem analysis in a couple of days. We'll take inventory of where we fell short. But even in this setback, there's a huge opportunity both for me and for the rep to make sure we don't make the same mistakes in the future. There's no time for blaming or complaining. Engaging in such activities avoids the issues and misses the opportunities.

Lack of Vision (I don't see.)

It's so interesting how things are connected. I was fortunate to earn a scholarship and play Division One collegiate soccer at Bowling Green State University. Looking back on my soccer career, there are things that are clear to me today that I didn't see when I failed to live with intention. I'll dive into this deeper soon, but I was one of those people who suffered from the "interference" I mentioned earlier, that Timothy Gallwey shined the light on. One example of how this interference and lack of vision affected my life occurred when my parents split up after my Freshman year of college. I was home to witness the end of their marriage, and it was hard to watch. But I swept the entire event under the rug. I lacked the vision to see what was possible if I acknowledged I was struggling, opened up to others, and pursued help. I kept everything inside and I didn't want to admit weakness.

Looking back, I now see the flaws in that approach. I realize the average collegiate athlete has about three and a half years in his or her career. That's not much time, and to make the most of it, focus is paramount.

Due to the sideways energy in my head and heart, I was blocked. Our brains and bodies are funny things. Amazing in

17

so many ways and, yet, so complicated in many more. When I say I was blocked, I mean the basic things became hard. I couldn't stay consistent. A bad touch to start a game and my negative thinking was off to the races. Doubt set in and created a compound effect. Bad touches became bad halves, bad games, and bad tournaments.

Lack of vision has this effect.

If we're not careful and intentional, our thoughts can get the best of us. It's a delicate balance, and it can turn on a dime. I could still perform at a reasonably high level from time to time, but overall, my ability to perform at key moments took a hit.

My confidence suffered the most because I lacked the vision to see a bright future. The rearview mirror got the best of me. It's no wonder—you can't create a bigger future when you keep focusing on mistakes in your past.

I call this tendency short-term thinking. When you're stuck and struggling, it's easy to get caught up in the moment. Making it through the next minute may be all you can muster.

There's no judgment coming from me. I get it. If we want to live with intention, however, we must transcend short-term thinking.

Getting called out on this might be the best thing for you. I know it was for me.

Back in 2014, I joined a mastermind. It was the morning of our in-person meetup, and we were headed to The Ohio State Reformatory—better known as the set of *The Shawshank Redemption*. Before we boarded the bus, our guest speaker, Chet Scott, author of *Becoming Built to Lead*, spoke to us. He challenged us about our inability to see clearly because of an obstacle blocking our path.

To illustrate the point, he held an iPad up with his left hand so we couldn't see his face. He talked about the blocks we each have and the messes we need to clean up to see clearly. We can't have a vision for the future unless we know the past and present blocks obstructing our view. It's only when we know the blocks and address them that our vision becomes clearer.

Chet is relentless about his clients' understanding and addressing their blind spots. Sure, there are times we simply can't see. At the beginning of the journey, most people don't know what's holding them back. They're called *blind* spots for a reason.

But that only goes so far.

Ignorance isn't bliss. There's a time to grow up and address the obstacles. Of course, it's painful. Chet calls this acute pain. Although acute pain is intense, it's momentary, intentional, and productive. Chronic pain is the pain that kills. It's constant and unproductive.

Most people choose lives of chronic pain. They don't want to address the bigger issue, and so they ignore it, avoid it, or distract themselves with a variety of vices. This is the very definition of someone living without intention. It might feel good at the moment, but the price tag is high and not worth the cost.

Lack of Discipline (I don't try.)

When I was a freshman in high school, I won a speech competition. Out of more than 200 students, I survived the gauntlet of judges and was crowned champion. My mom would wake up with me at 5:30 a.m., and we'd practice. I worked my butt off, rehearsing with her over and over again. She critiqued my cadence, my pauses, and my volume.

I committed to making this the best speech I would ever give. Looking back, I see the theme is humorous—a rendering of Little Red Riding Hood.

My English teacher, Brother Joe, wasn't sure what to think of it at first.. It was very different than the other speeches. One of my classmates performed a fiery rendition of General Patton's powerful speech to the Third Army before D-Day in Normandy.

The top three speeches in my class went on to compete against the rest of the top three from other classes. My speech landed me in the top three, but I didn't stop here. After this round, I prepared longer and harder, leaning on my mom to push me even more. She stepped up to the challenge, focusing on the nuances, inflections, and subtleties of my speech.

The discipline paid off, and I headed into the final round armed with confidence and competence. Brother Joe sensed my swagger, pulled me aside, and told me he thought I had the chops to be the first-ever four-time champion at the school.

Discipline has this effect, infusing us with self-belief. It prepares us to withstand a time of testing. But the opposite is true too. Lack of discipline leaves us faltering, dependent upon luck or chance. Other people sense our insecurity and respond with fear and doubt.

When you put in the work, usually, good things happen. The work doesn't guarantee success, but it sure puts you in a better position. The following year, I faltered. I got cocky and didn't invest as much time. I skipped the self-discipline, and the accolades skipped me.

I finished in third place that year.

I thought I had the speaking thing figured out. It came naturally to me, or so I thought. What I didn't realize until later in my professional career was that everything takes practice.

Those unseen hours. The time in the darkness. The hours of reps with my mom. Breaking down my speech to the smallest of pieces . . . everything mattered, all that effort. Discipline made me successful. All the preparation paid off. And in my moment of truth, when it came to performing the speech, I didn't have to think.

I let it fly.

My immature brain didn't get that at the time. Until I started going to Toastmasters in 2011, I never thought too much about working on speaking or preparing the way I did back in 1991 with my mom. I'll never forget her commitment to helping and encouraging me.

At some point, I stopped working on the craft of speaking. Those same mental blocks that tormented me in college soccer started showing up in the boardroom. My anxiety mounted in 2011, and although I was a former speech champion, I could no longer get my words out.

Panic attacks hijacked my brain, and I lost track of my thoughts.

It all caught up to me, but in the process, I learned a valuable lesson.

The work matters, and so does the preparation.

My friend Kary Oberbrunner says, "When you're prepared for the moment, the moment will be prepared for you."

He's right. Doing the work in the unseen hours matters.

Lack of Growth (I don't improve.)

I became a pretty good soccer player the same way I became a pretty good speaker—I was doing the work when no one was watching. I was putting in the work and growing.

The soccer part was easy because I loved the game. No one had to force me to practice. I loved waking up and knowing I had practice or a game. It was all I could think about. My mom and dad even installed a goal in our yard, so training every day all day was the norm.

Intentionality seemed to be a way of life. Growing was something I did naturally.

Then, as I mentioned, I got blocked. The interference set in. The mental struggles started—small as mustard seeds in the beginning. Ancient literature refers to the mustard seed as one of the most powerful seeds. These negative seeds were planted, small but mighty.

I stopped growing—and when you're not growing, you're dying.

I threw myself into alcohol, drugs, and girls. Anything that could get me through or distract from the angst.

Little by little, I found myself unable to perform on the field. Things like passing the ball became more challenging. I was an outside left midfielder. Getting a ball and crossing it in was kind of my specialty. But I got to the point where I couldn't execute the cross.

It got so bad that my coach required me to practice my crossing. He lined me up in front of the net and demanded that I crush the ball into the net—over and over again. It was embarrassing.

Crossing the ball wasn't my problem. It didn't result from a lack of skill or technique. Something much more significant was the problem—my head and my heart. I couldn't get into flow because I became my own critic. Constant judgment and analysis locked up my body and my brain. Psychologist Mihaly Csikszentmihalyi popularized the term *flow* in relation to a state of being that was the opposite of what I was experiencing. Here's how he describes it: "Flow is an optimal state of consciousness, a peak state where we both feel and perform our best. We become so involved in an activity that nothing else seems to matter. The ego falls away. Time flies. Every action, movement and thought follows inevitably from the previous one, like playing jazz. Your whole being is involved, and you're using your skills to the utmost." [3] There were many times in my career when I had accessed a flow state, but those days were over.

For the rest of my career, it became a struggle to stay on the field. I finished all four years, but I went from being a key contributor with a bright future to being the last guy off the bench in my final game my senior year in the NCAA Tournament.

I entered the game with about fifteen minutes left. We were losing 1–0 to Indiana University, the top team in the country. I had a chance to impact the game.

A ball came my way right after I got in. I was on the left side, as usual. I dribbled the ball into some space and now was my chance to cross the ball—and get the tying goal.

The ball left my foot, and I quickly realized I didn't follow through. It drifted right into the goalkeeper's hands. Chance averted. Redemption stalled.

We went on to lose that game 4–0.

The game was televised nationally on Fox. I kept a recording and watched it a couple of times after our season was over. Then a few years later, I found it again and promptly threw it away. No need to watch it anymore. My professional aspirations were now a distant memory. Even though I had a couple of minor league tryouts, mentally I was in no shape to play anymore.

* * *

Fast forward to my business career. My first panic attack bit me during a training I gave with a customer in Nashville a few years before my promotion to the sales role. I chalked it up to a bad day. I left the room in the middle of my presentation. The stakes were low. I got a drink, cleared my head, then came back and finished the training.

I looked as though I had it all together, but beneath the surface, I was a mess. You'd think I would've learned my lesson, but I didn't. Positive and put together on the outside but negative and crumbling on the inside. The anxiety surfaced every once in a while, but I managed to keep it together—that is, until I was promoted.

Looking back, I can't believe I made it five years before I completely bonked out. I'd have bouts of these mini attacks, but I became an expert at hiding. With the stakes raised, I had to present in front of bigger audiences, and there was much more on the line.

No one knew my battle, and I liked it that way. I resorted to status quo thinking and living. I now know experts call this a fixed mindset.

Carol Dweck, a pioneer in the now-popular topic of growth mindset, has much to say about this. In her book *Mindset*, she unpacks the differences between a fixed mindset and a growth mindset.

Those with a fixed mindset stay stuck in a "status quo" environment. They think they *can't* change, improve, or transform. On the flip side, growth mindset people never stop progressing. They know they *can* change, improve, and transform.

By now, you're probably starting to see how living without intention doesn't serve you or your future. Rest assured, good news is coming. But before we dive into how living *with* intention helps you and those around you, we first need to look at how living *without* intention affects others.

Warning. It's not pretty. But as we learned in this chapter from James Clear, "The process of behavior change starts with self-awareness."

On that topic, get ready for more self-awareness.

CHAPTER 2

LACK OF SERVING INTENTIONALLY (I CAN'T)

*Serving is a sign of intentional greatness,
not accidental weakness.*

No one stumbles upon significance. We have to
be intentional about making our lives matter.
—John Maxwell

In Chapter 1, we examined what we lack when we live without intention. These five components concern our relationship with *ourselves*:

1. Lack of Self-Awareness
2. Lack of Ownership
3. Lack of Vision
4. Lack of Discipline
5. Lack of Growth

Without Intention Wheel - Self

In Chapter 2, we'll examine five other components we lack when we live without intention. These five components concern our relationship with *others*:

1. Lack of Authenticity
2. Lack of Compassion
3. Lack of Creativity
4. Lack of Humility
5. Lack of Energy

Without Intention Wheel—Others

Lack of Authenticity (I can't be honest.)

No matter how far we try to run away from our demons, they'll haunt us until we deal with them. After college, although I didn't perform in soccer any longer, I was required to perform at a high level for work, often during account reviews.

It was my turn to speak in front of my peers. My mind went blank. I couldn't get the words out. My therapist had instructed me to fake a headache if this happened.

I moved to the side of the room and put my hand to my head. Some of my colleagues came over to see if I was okay. I said I needed to sleep and went up to my hotel room. Three hours later, I woke up and hoped it had all been a bad dream.

To my dismay, it wasn't.

Those same head games that beat me on the field came back to beat me in the boardroom. Something had to be done. I could no longer keep living a lie.

Fast forward several years to meeting Chet Scott that morning before visiting Shawshank. Chet runs a world-class leadership development firm called Built to Lead. He works with C-level executives, Olympic athletes, and top sports coaches.

He said a great deal that morning, but I only remember the part about needing to fix myself.

Later that day, we made our way up Interstate 71. Once we arrived at Shawshank, we engaged in a writing exercise. My friend Kary, the mastermind leader, gave us the opportunity to spend some time in our own prison cell—literally.

I walked into my cell and slid the cold, rusty bars shut. I sat on the crude metal bed frame and began to write. We were challenged to write a letter to our future selves—an encouragement letter of sorts.

I wrote a real letter, but I filled out a fake address. I guessed what Kary had planned to do with those letters—mail them back to us at a later date.

I rebelled.

I didn't want to be reminded of the truth. I wanted that letter—the only place I was completely honest— to get lost in the mail.

After all, I felt lost.

Sitting in that prison cell after already getting called out earlier in the day, I knew change was needed.

I had to figure it out. I had to save my family. I had to be the dad I'd always wanted to be.

I had to break, and I knew the price of brokenness would cost me greatly.

I threw my life into my family, my identity, and my career. It wasn't easy or a quick fix. I continued therapy.

Feeling the brokenness in that prison cell was probably the most important moment of my life. I had to go backward before I could go forward. I had to accept who I was so I could pursue who I was created to be. For the first time in my life, I decided to live with intention.

That's the goal of this book—to help you live and lead with intention. Until we do, our relationship with others will be transactional at best.

The truth is that most relationships are transactional. In the first few years of my sales career, I was more interested in what my customers could do for me than in what I could do for them. I was focused on the money and getting what I wanted. My success was fleeting. Sure, I had an occasional good year, but it wasn't consistent. It's almost embarrassing to write this as I think back.

Me, myself, and I. That's all I truly cared about— my reputation and my results.

I lived this "fake" life. I even faked myself out.

We all tend to live an inauthentic life. We shy away from being vulnerable. We buy the fancy car and the big house. We get the dog and the 2.3 kids. We get married and join the country club.

It can be a facade. I know because I was there.

People feel it, though. Looking back, I believe my customers felt I wasn't in it for them. Sure, I could befriend them and find some ways to help, but I was leading with a "me first" attitude.

Authenticity matters. Trust matters. Vulnerability matters. Transformational relationships in business and life matter. All of this begins by living with intention.

Lack of Compassion (I can't empathize.)

When my dad was dealing with his mental health challenges, he stayed in the hospital for a couple of weeks. Although things were off during that time, life went on. My brothers and I continued to go to school and play sports. Our parents were always super supportive, and they drove us to every game and practice. For a little while, my dad wasn't in his usual spot in the corner of the field shouting words of encouragement. He used to yell, "C'mon, Jon boy!" I could hear him in every game, but not for those two weeks. Then he returned and nothing changed—at least, on the surface.

Back to normal.

We swept it under the rug and never talked about it as a family. Most families don't talk about mental health. In fact, most communities and countries avoid the topic. Why, I'm not sure. We're comfortable talking about physical health issues but not mental ones.

Perhaps it's because we struggle with empathy. When we embody empathy, we put ourselves in someone else's shoes. We see the world from their perspective. We feel what they feel. It's not easy to do, and it takes work.

But our society seems to be shifting—in a good way. The stigma of mental health is losing its power, in part thanks to many high-profile athletes who are speaking out. In the sports world, guys like Kevin Love, Demar Derozan, and Michael Phelps have talked openly about their challenges.

In the 2021 Summer Olympics in Tokyo, Japan, Simone Biles pulled out of most competitions due to the "twisties"—a dangerous mental block for gymnasts. She could've broken her neck if she performed a move the wrong way, so instead, she pulled out. Many critics took to social media, labeling her a quitter and a fraud.

Biles was the number one gymnast in the world at the time by a long shot. Some called her one of the greatest Olympic champions of all time, if not *the* greatest. Think about the pressure that comes along with such a title. It's amazing that she performed the way she did for so long on the world's stage.

It's encouraging that Biles is openly speaking about this because her words and actions will save lives. The stats are mind-blowing. About 21 percent of U.S adults deal with diagnosable mental health challenges. [4] During the COVID-19 pandemic, these numbers shot up by 25 percent. [5]

Approximately 800,000 people worldwide take their own lives every year. This means over 2,000 people per day, roughly one death every 40 seconds.[6]

In the United States, we've seen a 30 percent increase in suicide from 2000–2020. Males represent almost 80 percent of these numbers. The experts think these incidents are underreported. It's scary stuff. But it's real, and we need to talk about it.

Living with intention means living with compassion. It means letting people know it's okay to not be okay.

Personally, everything changed when I was able to be open with my struggles.

If you're struggling, you're not alone. Ask for help. Talk to a friend, a coach, a teacher, a colleague, or a parent. I've discovered that people want to help. Everyone is going through something. Perhaps this is what popularized the saying "Be kind, for everyone you meet is fighting a hard battle."

I've found that most human beings feel compassion and empathy for others. By sharing your challenges, you might give someone else the courage to be open about theirs. I've seen this so many times. The more authentic you are with people, the more trust you will build.

Stigmas must change, and when we live with intention, they change faster. That's why writing this book isn't merely an academic exercise. My hope and prayer are that it might save a life—literally.

Lack of Creativity (I can't produce.)

I didn't understand for several years (despite having a career in sales) that producing a result for someone is a vital part of serving them. Maybe you're more attuned than I was.

It took me a while to realize that creating value is a missing piece of the equation in many human interactions. Many people struggle with being resourceful enough to figure out a way to produce a desired outcome.

I know I've been there.

I remember a big meeting I had with one of my key accounts. My manager and I were flying down to Atlanta to meet with two executives. I had one of our account support reps who specializes in data send me a report that I was going to present at this meeting. There were some issues that morning with the initial report, and she was making some updates for me.

We were at lunch with another client before the meeting, and I remember my manager saying he felt uneasy about the changes being made so close to the meeting time.

We showed up at the office with a few minutes to spare. I pulled up the slide deck—the format was completely jumbled. The deck looked like gibberish and everyone in the room knew it.

Needless to say, the meeting was a big miss. On our way back to the Atlanta airport, my manager put some music on and barely said a word to me. His silence was deafening. This was another example of me failing to deliver value. I never forgot that moment, and I vowed never to show up empty again. That day I committed to producing visible results and overdelivering for our clients and stakeholders.

Looking back, I see I should have rescued that failed presentation by being honest. Everyone in the room felt the awkwardness, and I should have owned it. Imagine if I would have been creative and used the time to discover more about the client and their needs rather than focusing on myself and my lack of performance.

Since that day, I've realized we're all flawed people, and the sooner we own it, the faster we can drop the masks and meet practical needs. We can't read minds or perform miracles—however, we can use what we have and be honest.

Maybe this is why stories like David and Goliath resonate so deeply.

David was offered the king's armor to fight the giant. He could have hidden his scrawny frame behind impressive state-of-the-art equipment. But he didn't— instead, he used what he had.

He relied on what he knew rather than what made sense to other people. His creative approach certainly caught his opponent off guard. Goliath might have mocked him for bringing a slingshot to a sword fight. Nevertheless, it's what led to his downfall and death. Malcolm Gladwell wrote an entire book, *David and Goliath*, about the power of having a "David mindset."

Once we get over ourselves—how we look and how we perform—then and only then do we have a chance to deliver true value. Up until that point, we're too self-consumed to focus on creating value for others.

Lack of Humility (I can't let go.)

We all have an ego. You're not going to rid yourself of it. But ego can be your servant or your master—just like pride. Pride can be good—or bad. Pride could help you do the extra work to get the job done. Did a parent or coach ever challenge you to take pride in your work?

But there's a paradox here.

Pride is the cause of many downfalls. Hitler had an ego problem. Napoleon too. You can probably insert most dynamic leaders into this equation. They probably struggled with pride.

Pride and ownership often go together. Michael Jordan had an ego. He was one of the fiercest competitors I've ever seen play. I'll never forget watching him play live in the 1998 NBA Finals.

His pride drove him. There are countless stories of how hard he competed at practice. He wanted to win at everything. That made him the greatest basketball player of all time.

Jordan was so good that his branded shoes still make him millions of dollars every year. My son, Gabe, loves a good sneaker, and Jordans are his favorite. Air Jordan 1 Retros to be exact. Think about it. A shoe from the 1980s is still relevant today. Gabe never saw Jordan play. Gabe was born in 2007 many years after Jordan retired. Yet Jordans are still the most popular shoes out there.

But take the flip side.

Jordan has struggled to succeed as an owner. His teams haven't reached anywhere near the heights of his playing days. He's also been mired in gambling controversies and conflicts with friends. I don't know him, and I have no idea what kind of person he is, but my hunch is that his ego and pride—the same ego and pride that won him championships—have a dark side too.

Bestselling author Ryan Holiday is spot on: "Ego is the enemy."

And humility is the answer.

This doesn't mean you can't be confident. Too much humility isn't good either—at least humility without belief. It's a fine line, but one that can take you to the next level in whatever it is you're trying to accomplish.

Remember, humility is not thinking less of yourself—it's thinking of yourself less.

Lack of Energy (I can't keep up.)

We live under constant attack—the buzzing of our phones keeps us in an elevated state of stress. This is neither good nor healthy.

When I was at the bottom and struggling to keep things together, my energy levels were not good. I could fake it for a bit, but it was a constant struggle. When I'd take clients out to dinner, I would chug a Red Bull before dinner started and then top it off with more Red Bull mixed with vodka—a recipe for disaster.

I had so much garbage built up through the years I was in survival mode, and I didn't even realize it. Survival mode leads to selfishness. When you're battling to survive, your primary focus is yourself.

Have you been there?

Maybe you're there now.

If so, give yourself a little grace.

It's hard to focus on others if you're struggling to make it through the day. Remember, time is a finite resource. Energy isn't.

I've studied and put into play many different productivity hacks and systems, from David Allen's *Getting Things Done* to Stephen Covey's *First Things First* (and many more in between). They all have their place, but most models overlook one key component—energy.

You can be the most efficient and productive person, but at what cost?

Tony Schwartz and Jim Loehr have spent a lot of time studying this. They are pioneers in the field of energy management vs. time management. In their research, they took a group of executives at Wachovia Bank (now part of Wells Fargo) through a program of energy renewal and management.

In their work, they conducted energy audits where each participant answered sixteen questions related to energy management. These focused on four components: body, emotions, mind, and spirit. On average, these participants got more than half of the answers incorrect—they were eating poorly, failing to express gratitude to others, practicing extreme multitasking, and failing to spend time on things that give them a sense of purpose.

The research showed that when these executives were intentional about things like eating for energy, prioritizing rest as much as work, breathing exercises, etc., they found greater levels of success and lower levels of stress.

In my research, I've found much of the same. I've interviewed many executives, top-level sports coaches, high-level sales leaders, and reps. The vast majority struggle with proper sleep and energy management. Although some produce impressive results, this comes at a steep cost.

Living without intention isn't a life worth emulating. In the next chapter, we'll unpack the three outcomes of intention deficit disorder.

CHAPTER 3

THREE OUTCOMES OF INTENTION DEFICIT

By living without intention, we've intentionally chosen to fail.

Pain is inevitable. Misery is a choice.
—Christopher Reeve

L iving with intention yields a big payoff. Three big outcomes, actually:

1. Results
2. Influence
3. Fulfillment

These will be our focus for the remainder of the book—a deep dive into living with intention. First, however, we need to close the loop on living without intention. The stakes are high, and there's a price to pay. Living without intention means experiencing the following:

1. Lack of Results
2. Lack of Influence
3. Lack of Fulfillment

How do I know?

Simple. I've experienced it firsthand, and it's not pretty. I've talked about my struggles thus far for a reason. I'm committed to full transparency because nobody benefits when we sugarcoat the truth.

Knowing where you are today and what may be holding you back is very important. Identifying where you're lacking is the first step to creating a bigger and brighter future.

In my career, I went from almost being fired to serving as a top-tier sales rep and eventually being promoted to lead a team. I've even been honored with the opportunity to teach the With Intention process to our entire company.

It's surreal, and I don't take it for granted. I am grateful and blessed. I've had key people pull me aside and tell me my transformation is unbelievable. My friend Naved, another leader at our company, said this to me one time, and I kind of chuckled.

Was I that bad before? Maybe so. That's okay.

I know I have much further to go. We all do. And if my failures help you on your journey to success, then it was all worth it.

On that topic, let's jump in with the final three "lacks."

Lack of Results (I am not contributing.)

Wherever you work and whatever you do, I imagine there is some type of result tied to it. If you're a sales leader or rep, you have a number or metric you track for customer success.

In my role, we track our NPS (net promoter score). It's a benchmark for how our customers feel about us. Essentially, we're asking if they would recommend us. We've been fortunate to grow this over time and now have a high NPS—in the eighty range—which ranks us among the best companies in the world. This is due to a relentless approach to how we serve our customers.

We measure and embody a mindset of service.

Do we always get it right? Absolutely not.

But we're quick to course correct when we don't.

Over time, we've been able to get it right more often than not, and we feel good about the way we're contributing to our customers' success.

With my particular team, we talk incessantly about customer service and adding value every day. It's a mindset. I try to embody this when I talk to my team. I make it a point to give them my full attention. Sometimes we talk for five minutes. Other times we talk for two hours. My purpose as a leader is to serve them and help them serve our customers.

When you're not getting the results you set out to achieve, it can be hard. You invest a ton of work with no visible success. It's frustrating for anyone.

I get it, but here's the silver lining.

Eventually, the score takes care of itself.

I get this line from Bill Walsh's book by the same name: *The Score Takes Care of Itself*. Walsh coached the San Francisco 49ers in the eighties to multiple Super Bowl wins. To do so, he needed to turn around a terrible franchise in only three years. His motto was simple: do the right things the right way on a consistent basis and the rest will take care of itself.

He focused on how the players dressed and how they treated the janitor at their practice facility. He believed everything mattered, and he made it a point to do everything with excellence.

Guess what happened to the 49ers in a few short years— the results manifested over time, and they earned multiple championships.

Lack of Influence (I am not important.)

The other night, I was sitting on my back patio watching my twelve-year-old daughter, Reese, teaching my eight-year-old daughter, Emerson, how to play lacrosse. For at least an hour, Reese was coaching Emerson on the intricacies of holding a lacrosse stick and cradling the ball so it doesn't fall out. She even put her through a drill where she would roll the ball out and Emerson would have to beat her to the ball and scoop it up. If you've never tried this, by the way, it's harder than you would think. It takes quite a bit of practice to get proficient with a lacrosse stick and ball.

I was a proud dad. These two have plenty of fights, like most siblings. I took some videos and pictures, and I'm sure I will cherish that moment for years to come.

Two things came from this little encounter. Emerson pretty much fell in love with lacrosse in one hour. The fact that her big sis was teaching her meant so much to her. She begged and begged the next day for her own stick. My wife took her to Dick's Sporting Goods, and they got a stick and some goggles. She's all in now.

But here's the other thing that happened. I could see Reese's confidence oozing when they finished. It felt good for her to teach her little sister. Lacrosse is fairly new to Reese as well—she's only in her second year. Teaching someone else always makes you better.

This is influence in its purest form.

Reese influenced Emerson. First, she talked her into practicing. Then she captured her attention for at least an hour. The experience proved so engaging that she inspired Emerson to request her own equipment.

Let's be honest—we all want to be viewed as important and successful. Everybody is an influencer. Everybody is in sales. Even our kiddos.

It's painful when we lack influence. For starters, it gives our ego a hit, but it also sets us back from believing we can achieve bigger and better goals. Our ability to influence others positively touches something deep inside us, creating lasting significance.

Lack of Fulfillment (I am not fulfilled.)

In 2016, our pastor brought in a guest speaker. This blonde surfer-looking dude with a white belt started talking, and right away, I remembered who he was. His name is Dustin, and I played soccer against him in college. He's one of those guys you can't forget. I hadn't thought about him until that day.

He started talking about an organization he started in Charlotte, North Carolina, called Project 658. It was inspired by a Bible verse from the Gospel of John—chapter 6 verse 58: "This is the bread that came down from heaven . . . whoever feeds on this bread will live forever."

His organization served the refugee community in Charlotte. They used sports (primarily soccer) to forge relationships and also taught these refugees basic skills like cooking and sewing so they could find work in the United States.

Dustin talked about God using people who may seem insignificant to do big things. He referenced another Bible passage where a little boy's lunch was used to feed many people. Dustin invited us to come on a mission trip to serve. He wanted families to participate together. I was in from the moment he opened his mouth. Our family went to a meeting after church that day to learn more.

At that meeting, our pastor, David, asked who would be interested in volunteering to lead.

I raised my hand. Our family served that year, and I had the privilege of co-leading the trip for three years.

I learned a valuable lesson about fulfillment. It was hot in Charlotte in June each year. I mean so hot that you started sweating the moment you went outside. We took about forty people on this trip, and I can't even name one time when anyone complained. There were little kids and senior citizens.

Everyone was all-in.

The light bulb moment for me was a day when I took my watch off and left my phone in the car. I served as best I could for a couple of hours with my family and our friends.

Present.

Intentional.

Fulfilled.

On that trip, I learned life is full of blessings and battles, and both are part of the journey.

Sometimes it's easier to remain present on a trip. Back in my hometown, life happens. Work happens. I'm not immune to the hamster wheel or the constant bombardment of emails, texts, and other notifications.

What about you?

Do you have moments of joy?

Are you truly fulfilled?

Intention deficit disorder is real, and it comes with a cost. To experience more fulfillment, you must take action. Sometimes that's removing the bad things from your life—or the bad people who bring you down. Sometimes it's finding new passions and new friends or new experiences.

Many times it's dying to yourself and your ego—choosing selflessness, choosing purpose.

As you know, life is a series of ups and downs. It's full of blessings and battles. But I can assure you from personal experience that you can find true fulfillment even in those battles.

If you've felt any pain reading this book so far, then congrats—you're human. Pain unites us all.

Be encouraged. Even though the truth hurts, the truth also sets us free.

The rest of this book leads you to that truth—the With Intention path.

PART 2
THE PATH

With Intention

CHAPTER 4

BUILD YOURSELF (I DO)

You can't lead someone further than you've led yourself.

How long can you afford to put off who you really want to be? Separate yourself from the mob. Decide to be extraordinary and do what you need to do—now.

—Epictetus

Y ou need to build yourself first.

That may sound a bit selfish, but let me explain. I'm a firm believer in the servant leadership mindset, but how do you serve others if you're not serving yourself?

Think about the wisdom found in so much ancient literature, including the Bible.

"Love your neighbor as yourself" (Luke 10:27).

It sounds to me like loving yourself and serving yourself is a given. Then and only then will we have something left to give to others.

You know the airplane analogy: in case of an emergency put your mask on first, then help the person next to you. Some people seem to get it backward. They don't practice self-care. They burn out, and then they wonder why they have nothing left to give to others.

We'll get into the serving piece in a bit, but let's focus first on building yourself. Like most principles in this book, it requires intentionality.

Building yourself is a never-ending process. Think of it as a flywheel. The best-selling author of *Good to Great*, Jim Collins, describes a flywheel as a wheel that takes significant force to get moving, however, with steady and consistent effort, it eventually starts to generate momentum and turn itself.

Our flywheel in this book is the With Intention Wheel.

With Intention Wheel - Self

Notice the five components:

1. **Awareness**: Knowledge of your current state
2. **Agency**: Taking ownership of your current state
3. **Ambition:** Seeing your future state
4. **Action:** Closing the gap between your current state and future state
5. **Adjustment**: Changing the direction on your way to your future state

These five components changed my life for the better, but not only my life. I've also seen firsthand how the With Intention Wheel changed other people's lives too, both personally and professionally.

I wish I'd discovered this framework sooner because I wouldn't have missed as many opportunities. Hindsight is always 20/20, isn't it? As the saying goes, although the best time to plant a tree was twenty years ago, the second-best time is today.

So what are we waiting for? Time to get started.

Awareness (I know.)—Identify your personal blind spots and professional gaps so you can step into your genius and make your time count.

In 2011, as I was rebuilding my speaking confidence, I attended a Toastmasters meeting. If you're not familiar with the organization, Toastmasters helps speakers train and get better. It's a safe environment where you practice many different kinds of speeches.

In your first speech, you're supposed to talk about yourself for three to five minutes. Easy-peasy. No need for notes—just get up and talk, right? Not me. I had my notes written down. I got up in front of the room, swaying from side to side. I remember my hands shaking.

Shoot! Everyone noticed the shaking, right? I was too busy staring at my notes to know for sure. My internal temperature rose like the anxiety within me.

I knew fear in a fresh, unfiltered way.

I vowed to get through, as clunky as it felt. This was my path toward redemption after the corporate panic attack I'd experienced a few months earlier. Embrace the fear was my motto.

No one needed to tell me my flaws; I was self-aware, maybe too aware. On a physical level, when I would speak, my body felt warm. My neck tightened, and I even experienced a choking sensation at times

Ever watch a sporting event where the team is on the field during the national anthem? If so, you'll see plenty of players getting their pre-game jitters out. Some athletes bounce up and down. Others do stretches. Some remain remarkably calm.

Me, when I played? I was the guy shaking his legs around on the field You can't do this in the boardroom without looking weird. If you try, I'm pretty sure the other people would look at you kind of funny. Once in a while, as I'd feel my nerves settling in, I'd leave to go to the bathroom. I'd take a breather, get a drink of water, and pace around the room a bit.

I didn't want to live out the rest of my professional career like this. I had enough self-awareness to know there had to be a better way. I'd find that way, and I knew attending Toastmasters and getting through that first speech would be a step in the right direction.

* * *

At this point in our With Intention journey, maybe I've earned the right to ask you a simple question.

Do you know yourself?

Maybe you're thinking, *Dumb question, Jon! Of course, I know myself.*

But let me ask again, do you really know yourself? Do you understand your strengths, weaknesses, and blind spots?

Do you know what people say about you when you're not in the room?

This list goes on and on. There are a million different ways to slice it, but insatiable curiosity about yourself is crucial, and it takes serious work.

See if this makes sense. I'm going to build out a model so you can visualize it. Imagine X is your starting point. Of course, you want to get better. We all do. Y is the goal state, usually up and to the right. There's rarely ever a straight line to get from X to Y. You'll have obstacles along the way and it's vital that you figure out what those are. Blind spots as well. Gaining awareness on both obstacles and blindspots is crucial.

51

Obstacles

Let's talk about obstacles first. Everything up to this point in your life has led you to today. I knew I had a lot of stuff holding me back. These were obstacles. But as we discovered at the beginning of the book, knowing and doing are two different things. We called this gap between knowing and doing the performance gap.

Blind Spots

Then there's the stuff we don't see. This is different than obstacles. Obstacles are in front of us, but blind spots are invisible to us. Unawareness is kryptonite because we can't improve what we can't perceive. Other people see our blind spots, but we don't, and oftentimes we don't want to see them or even hear about them.

Remember a few chapters back when I told the story about receiving those phone calls that impacted my largest accounts? I complained to my new boss about the raw deal I received and how the client was to blame. Then, my boss quickly informed me about my blind spot. He said, "Jon, where there's smoke there's fire." Remember that story?

Ouch. He clearly showed me a blind spot—a lack of awareness. From that moment on, I didn't complain about what happened. My boss gave me a gift that day. He told me the truth and shone a light on my blind spot. If you have truth tellers like this in your life, thank them! They bring awareness, and on the other side of awareness, there's always greatness.

The With Intention Awareness© Matrix

I'm a visual learner, so I created the With Intention Awareness (WIA) Matrix. It depicts the relationship between competence and awareness. High competence is a strength.

Low competence is a weakness.

High awareness is an asset.

Low awareness is a liability

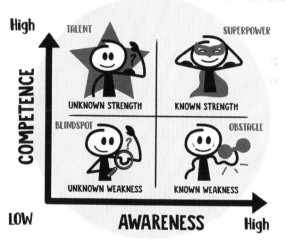

Here's a deeper look:

- **Unknown Weakness—Blind Spot (Low Competence / Low Awareness):** The lower-left quadrant is an unknown weakness, otherwise known as a blind spot. This is something you aren't aware of, and there's a good chance it's holding you back. It's very important to gain awareness here.

- **Known Weakness—Obstacle (Low Competence / High Awareness):** The lower-right quadrant is a known weakness. With this knowledge, you can focus on improving your weakness, delegating it, or mitigating it in some way.

- **Unknown Strength—Talent (High Competence / Low Awareness):** The upper-left quadrant is an unknown strength. There's often gold here. Trusted advisors can help you "mine" this talent and leverage it to create visible results in work and life. So, it's not yet cultivated but there's a big opportunity here.

- **Known Strength—Superpower (High Competence / High Awareness):** The upper-right quadrant is your sweet spot. You know your strength. You live it. When you use your superpower, you're in flow. You feel the effects and so do the people around you. This is one you want to lean into.

* * *

Now, that we've framed up the different types of awareness, let's dive into some ways to learn about yourself. One tool I highly recommend is a 360. It's an assessment where you solicit feedback from others. We tend to be myopic—we only see what we want to see. Anaïs Nin expounded upon this tendency when she said, "We don't see things as they are, we see them as we are."

Our perspective is hardly the full picture. We benefit from other people's feedback. In her book *Insight,* organizational psychologist Tasha Eurich emphasizes this point. She defines self-awareness as "the ability to see ourselves clearly—to understand who we are, how others see us, and how we fit into the world."[7]

Agency (I care.)—Take complete ownership of your past and present so your focus stops getting "hacked."

People living with intention take appropriate responsibility in work and life. This is the definition of agency—taking ownership, especially when there's an opportunity to improve.

Think back to my example of working in sales when I realized I was being selfish. Once I became self-aware, I had the choice to take ownership and make improvements.

Notice how awareness precedes agency. Referencing the illustration below, once I see myself accurately at X and have the desire to move to Y, I have the choice to take ownership.

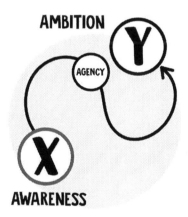

This was the same pattern I experienced with my speaking and panic attacks. Rather than run from them, I chose to take ownership. As a result, I embodied agency by signing up for Toastmasters.

This experience became the safe environment I needed to keep improving. Although it was painful in the beginning, eventually I moved from X to Y and gained confidence in the process. Week after week on Thursday mornings I woke up around 6 a.m. and visited Tim Horton's for an egg sandwich and a coffee on the way to Vineyard Church where the gatherings took place. I did my reps, exactly as I had back in the day with my mom when I practiced Little Red Riding Hood. The experience stretched me, but it also built me. By practicing agency, I demonstrated care about the bigger future I was creating.

The same was true at work. After losing much of my book of business, I had no choice but to start over. I knew I had it in me, but I still had to make the conscious choice to take ownership. The cool part is that both situations—the speaking and the sales—helped each other. With each step in the process and each move toward a greater sense of agency, one would feed off the other. I started to feel more confident at meetings, and with a newfound focus on serving our customers and helping our team produce, changes were set in motion.

It's amazing what happens when you take ownership. People step up to help. As I got more honest about the issues I struggled with, several colleagues expressed a genuine interest in helping me. As I got better, I returned the favor. Together we all became stronger. Our entire team started performing at a higher level.

* * *

What about you?

Is there an area you're now aware of needing to improve?

I know it's not always easy, especially in the beginning. Maybe you have something holding you back. What if you were able to take ownership and unlock this struggle? Would you get closer to tapping into your God-given gifts and potential?

One of the best things I ever learned was from a coach who had me draw a circle.. Let me explain.

I was complaining about something in my life. (Big shocker. I wasn't living with intention yet.)

David, my coach at the time, interrupted my complaining and asked me to get a pen. Then he asked me to draw a big circle and put a smaller circle inside the bigger one. Then he asked me to shade in the smaller circle.

I looked at the drawing, a bit perplexed.

Then he said, "Jon, you can only control the smaller circle. The rest is just noise. Focus on what you can influence and you can grow this over time"

This lightbulb moment is one I revisit often.

Your Shaded Circle

Stephen Covey popularized this circle-in-a-circle concept in *The 7 Habits of Highly Effective People.* I read it many years ago and forgot about it until David brought it back to my memory. These days, I find myself advising people on this concept all the time— control what you can control.

I even coach myself on the concept. Like most people, when life shows up, there are times I forget the simple but profound truths.

As we steward our influence well, our influence increases. Our job is to expand that small circle by focusing on what's inside it.

When something happens to you, ask yourself, "What can I control? How will I respond?"

Maybe the answer is an attitude, a mindset, or an action. This little exercise is a game changer because when you take ownership and focus only on what you can influence, everything else changes.

Ready to give it a try?

If so, stop right now and think of something on your mind. Maybe it's causing you a bit of stress. Now think about one thing you can do to influence the situation.

I don't care how small that one thing is. No judgment.

Here's a personal example. Throughout the journey of writing this book, it was difficult for me to write at times. I dealt with many fits and starts. Sometimes I got stuck and ended up letting weeks pass without writing a word. I let perfection hack my brain, aiming for flawlessness.

Every time I talked to my publisher he told me to simply keep writing. "Put words on a page. Stop critiquing and editing. Just create, no matter how big or small."

I listened to his advice. I would sit my butt in the seat and open my laptop and start writing. When I did, good things happened, and I made progress. Of course, my words didn't flow perfectly, but I took ownership and controlled my "small shaded circle." When I did, the process left me feeling empowered. My influence increased, and lo and behold, I completed the book.

So what is it for you? What's the one thing you can do right now to influence your situation? Take that step. That's ownership. That's agency.

I know taking ownership isn't always easy. And I'm not about pumping you up with a fake positivity message—optimism for optimism's sake. I'm hoping you choose realism over pessimism. There's a big difference.

We all know pessimism can kill you. Guess what—so can false optimism. This is why I lean toward realism.

Check out this true story about Admiral Jim Stockdale, a United States POW in Vietnam. From 1965 to 1973, he was tortured relentlessly without a release date. He had no idea if he'd ever see his family again.

Jim Collins, author of *Good to Great*, interviewed Stockdale. When Collins asked him how he made it through, Stockdale said, "I never lost faith in the end of the story." He went on to say, "I never doubted not only that I would get out, but also that I would prevail in the end and turn the experience into the defining event of my life, which, in retrospect, I would not trade."

Collins asked him who didn't make it out, and here was Stockdale's response, "Oh, that's easy. The optimists. Oh, they were the ones who said, 'We're going to be out by Christmas.' And Christmas would come, and Christmas would go. Then they'd say, 'We're going to be out by Easter.' And Easter would come, and Easter would go. And then Thanksgiving, and then it would be Christmas again. And they died of a broken heart."

Stockdale finished with a somber warning: "This is a very important lesson. You must never confuse faith that you will prevail in the end . . . with the discipline to confront the most brutal facts of your current reality, what they might be."[8]

Stockdale is right. Possessing a brutally honest view of where you are today and taking complete ownership are two essential steps required for any significant breakthrough.

Ambition (I see.): Create a new future that reflects your ideal legacy.

My journey toward being able to speak confidently again started with a vision. I kept picturing myself on a stage somewhere with the audience in front of me and lights shining in my face. I'd often say to myself, *What if you could turn this around, rebuild your confidence, and become who you were called to be?*

During this process, I joined a coaching cohort based on Kary Oberbrunner's book *The Deeper Path*. This book outlined a process called OPUS based on a framework created by Chet Scott, the same guy who called me out the morning we went to Shawshank.

OPUS stands for

O = Overarching Vision
P = Purpose
U = Unifying Strategies
S = Scorecard for Success

Chet and Kary have coached hundreds of people through this process. I'm a client and friend of both coaches. I know this works because I get to live it out daily.

One exercise Kary challenged us to do was create our "I have a dream" speech. He based it on Martin Luther King Jr.'s example and challenged us to be bold and hold nothing back. This was the first time I put something in writing about my future and learned how powerful vision was.

At this point, I was getting my "sea legs" in terms of speaking. I certainly wasn't perfect, but each time I spoke, I broadcasted more confidence. Work didn't slow down, and I presented consistently, doing more and more reps.

In my "dream speech," I talked about inspiring people and helping them reach their potential. Part of this plan included speaking on stages all across the world. I remember getting emotional as I read my speech from the front of the room. I'm not sure I fully believed this bigger future coming out of my mouth, but I verbalized it, nonetheless.

There's something powerful about putting an idea down on paper. Of course, we all have ambitions. And if you're like most people, you're thinking thousands of thoughts per day. Some of these thoughts are about your vision for the future.

Have you put these thoughts down on paper, though?

One of the most powerful things you can do is to write out a future state. But here's the secret most people don't know—you should write as though it's already happened.

Don't use phrases like "I will . . . I hope . . . I want . . ."

Use phrases like "I am . . . I have . . . I did . . ." instead.

So you might as well talk about your future as though it's already happened. When you do, you make your desires, aspirations, and goals that much more attainable.

I have a former soccer teammate and friend whom I now advise. He reached out to me about taking his company to the next level and some challenges he was facing. Early on in our conversations, I had him do a vision exercise. I gave him the following assignment:

> Put yourself exactly where you are this weekend, but ten years down the road. Look back on the prior ten years and write about what's transpired. How do you feel? What is your family like? What has your company accomplished? What impact have you created? Write it all out as though it's already happened. Be bold. Don't judge. Rather, just write. . . .

Here's what he wrote:

July 3, 2031

As I look back on the last ten years, I think about the impact both I and the company have had on so many people. First and foremost, my family. We currently live in San Diego. We bought this place about six years ago in Carmel Valley overlooking the ocean. It has five bedrooms and four bathrooms.

I ride my bike to work and surf in the morning. The kids are both at great schools and play sports. My daughter is seventeen and about to graduate high school. She will attend Stanford University and currently spends time working on the sustainability side of the business. She works with the forest service on wildlife sustainability.

My son is fifteen and playing soccer. He has been selected for the top team in San Diego. He's a sponsored skier and spends time at our place in Idaho in the summer and winter.

One of our highlights was that three generations were able to attend the Super Bowl in 2023 where the Browns beat the Chargers to win it all. We also all went to the World Cup in 2026 and watched the US team beat Brazil.

My wife and I share our time between San Diego and Idaho to spend time together and do the things we love. In 2024, we built a house on land we bought in Driggs, ID, back in 2021. The place is modern with incredible views of the Tetons. We have a few horses and a cow named Barley on the property.

I got my pilot's license, and we keep our Cessna Caravan 208B at a hangar close to the house to make it easier to get in and out of Driggs. My company was recognized as number one in the world for our commitment to sustainability as well as personal growth for employees and guides. The guide school, which was started in 2018, is now recognized nationally as the only accredited guide school in the nation and receives over one thousand applicants each year. We received the innovation in sustainability award at the PURE Life Experiences show in Morocco.

Over the past ten years, both businesses have grown considerably, and we now have sixty employees with offices in Alaska, Idaho, California, and Arizona for the US and Santiago, Chile, in South America. The camping business has exploded with ten new destinations, and in 2023 it received a $1M investment from one of our top clients.

The camp has been featured in *Forbes* Magazine as well as all the major travel magazines (*Travel & Leisure, Departures, Condé Nast, Afar*). It's the most sought-after experience in the country. My long-time business partner transitioned to exclusively managing the camping product that he helped create. In 2024, he was full-time on that operation.

The camping product, which had revenues of $700k in 2021, is now exceeding $10M per year in sales with operations across the county and over five thousand bed nights per year. The camping product was purchased in 2029 by a luxury hotel brand for $25M as a way to offer their guests luxury experiences when their properties are full, both to add capacity and to continue their innovative strategy to add luxury everywhere in the world.

We have continued to expand our offerings and marketing with a team of people focused on the client experience and daily delivery of each trip. I stopped guided trips in 2024 to start building my place in Driggs. Now I personally do only one trip for my long-standing clients (both corporate and personal). I have watched their families grow over the years and still stay close to them.

We have a separate arm of the business that focuses exclusively on retreats and creative experiences. My brother manages this side of the company and has grown its revenue and client base by 30% annually since 2022.

Our creative concepts have been covered by top industry publications as the new way the elite travel. We have transformed travel in this space and have done *James Bond, Pirates of the Caribbean, West World, Goonies, Indiana Jones,* and several new concepts. I am now responsible for sales and marketing, and our system and team deliver all the experiences we run each year.

We host over eight hundred trips a year with revenue exceeding $40M annually. We have an arm of the business that focuses on sustainability, and over the last ten years have been able to put kids through school on the Navajo reservation in the Four Corners area, created the first fully green travel option, and eliminated all waste from our camping product. We maintain a strong working culture where fun, creativity, innovation, and excellence are the pillars of what we do every day. The team meets in person four times a year; two of those are at off-site locations to discuss our strategy for new products and create new ways to deliver experiences. In addition to the growth of luxury travel, we have also been approached by several new luxury lodges and venues to create their experience packages and train their staff on how to create unique experiences for their guests.

I and some of the long-standing guides head this up. Today marks the first day of retirement for me, and I am taking the rest of the summer to sail from Mission Beach, Australia, to Sydney for four months with my family before our kids go off to college.

* * *

There's a lot here and I thought it was important to give you a good feel for how this works. What did you notice with this?

The main thing that sticks out to me—the most important piece—is he's writing it as though it already happened. He's also very detailed. Although it's ten years down the road, it feels like reality.

Will my friend reach his vision?

My hunch from working closely with him is that he's going to get pretty darn close and may even exceed it. Of course, circumstances will change, and it won't play out exactly as he wrote it. But writing out a clear vision and discovering his true ambitions will get him moving in the right direction. I know, I know—the Browns are unlikely to win the Super Bowl in 2023 (I'm also a long-suffering Browns fan!). But you get the point.

How about you? Want to give it a try?

It might be a bit scary. I get it. But what do you have to lose? You can articulate your vision in any time frame you want: one year, five years, ten years, twenty-five years, or more!

When I participated in a *7 Habits of Highly Effective People* training a few years back, they had us do a similar exercise visualizing our eightieth birthday party. We wrote about what people were saying about us and what impact we'd created for other people.

Think about that for a second. What do you want your children to say about you? How about your grandchildren? Your spouse or significant other? Your coworkers? Friends? Brothers or sisters?

This type of visioneering is incredibly powerful.

You're busy. So am I. Last time I checked, everyone was. However, are you making time for what's most important? Building a vision for your bigger future is your most important work.

Remember our simple illustration below? Remember, Y is your future state, your ambition. It's what you see.

AMBITION

AWARENESS

Do you know your Y? If not, let's get to work. Let's talk about goals a little bit.

I'll give an example from my context since you know my story. While transforming my career as a sales rep, I simplified everything. I still had a number to hit each year, and I needed to grow my book of business. I had a renewed focus on serving our customers and adding value first but I still had a vision in mind for what my targets were.

If my book of business was $5 million and my goal was to grow the book by 10 percent for the year, that would mean I needed to bring in an additional $500,000 in business.

The goal was simple—grow the business from $5 million to $5.5 million by 12/31/xx (end of the year). Although I'd used this type of framework in the past, Chris McChesney and Sean Covey codified it for me in their book *Four Disciplines of Execution*. I highly recommend it. This X to Y concept is inspired by them.

My vision (my Y) was front and center on my whiteboard in the office. I saw it daily. With each deal, my vision (my Y) was becoming a reality.

People tend to overcomplicate things. Keep it simple. What's your X to Y by when?

Take some time to write about this. Where do you want to go? And when? We'll cover more of this in the With Intention Plan at the end of this book. Together we'll build an intentional systematic approach.

For now, let's clarify your standards.

Standards

Everyone has standards. They serve as your operating system, the core tenets of who you are and how you work and live. Most people aren't aware of their standards. Rather than choosing them intentionally, they simply arrive at them by accident. Maybe their upbringing influenced them. Or maybe they accepted what was handed to them by others.

The OPUS process helped me clarify my standards. Chet Scott calls this your CORE. Similar to your physical core—the muscles that hold everything together—your internal CORE is the set of principles that holds you together.

These questions will help you think through your internal CORE:

- What do you believe and why?
- What do you value and why?
- What's important to you?
- What do you love to do?
- What do you hate to do?

If you want to live with intention, you need to clarify your standards. This process took me a while, and even after I wrote them down, I edited them over and over again. Reflecting on them now feels great. Living them in my daily life feels even greater. Remember, it's not about perfection but imperfect progress. Creating your standards is something I highly recommend. Mine have developed over time and it's a continuous process. Feel free to use this as inspiration for yours.

My Core

I've listed a handful of the standards in my core. For a complete list, reference the appendix.

- **Awake and present.** I'm tuned in and grateful. I know and understand we're all works in progress. Every day, every moment is a gift. It's also a challenge to remain awake.
- **There is always a way.** Elite performers are resourceful.
- **Take calculated risks.**
- **Keep it simple**. Complexity kills.
- **Brick by brick**. Put in the work and grow over time. Compound interest is real. Stop planning so much and start working.
- **Iterate as you go**. Commitment + iteration leads to results.
- **Lead with your heart**. The heart forms before your brain. It has its own intelligence system.
- **Clarity attracts**. Confusion repels.
- **Every achievement requires a key ingredient: energy.** What energy are you bringing to yourself and others every moment of every day?
- **Serve others** authentically.

- **Meaning matters**. Staying true to your purpose is crucial.

- **Seize the day**. Seize the opportunity in front of you.

- **Start with *why***. The tyranny of *how* holds me back. Start with the outcome and reason why, always. "Reasons come first, answers come second" (Jim Rohn).

- **Transforming by the day.** Incremental, continuous improvement is the focus. Miracles and magic leaps are rare. Focus on moving in the right direction. I am getting better daily. Today is a new day. Regardless of what happened yesterday, keep getting better today. Learn from down times and down weeks as much as great days and weeks. I have a relentless desire to get better.

- **Intentional and purpose driven**. I think about where I'm headed and the why behind it. I don't just *do*. Action needs to go in the right direction. Speed + direction = velocity. The right things deserve laser focus and intentional velocity. I'm purposeful with my actions, and they're aligned with my beliefs.

- **A catalyst and encourager**. My fuel comes from building into others. This is a gift I've been given; it's natural. I look for opportunities and moments to inspire, encourage, challenge, and awaken those in my path. **Comfortable with adversity**. It's going to happen, and it's about my ability to adjust and adapt, trusting in the work I've done and the mindset I've developed. The obstacle is the way. Life is full of blessings and battles. My ability to deal with both is a difference maker.

- **Deeply curious.** I am genuinely interested in people. What drives them is important to me. I want to learn about them—why they do what they do, what their journey is, what makes them tick, what their fears are, how they overcome their fears, and what legacy and story they're writing. Not surface-level stuff. I want them to feel heard and loved. This is what deep-seated, transformational relationships are about. I ask more questions than most, and that's a good thing.

- **A truth-seeker and believer.** I believe in a great God and the cross of Jesus. The great news of the gospel transformed my life on 10/21/15. I live with a purpose and the salt and light of that gift. Increasingly, not perfectly.

- **Focused on what I can influence.** There are always things that are going to be of concern and cause stress. The real question is this— what's in my control and what can I influence? My brain is wired to focus on the stressor. This doesn't have control over me. I own it and control what I can take action on.

Action (I try.)—Leverage the right mindset so you can win more days and achieve your vision.

Nothing matters unless you take action. You can be locked in with awareness, agency, and ambition, but this is where the rubber meets the road. The gap. This is what you're trying to close—the space between where you are today and where you want to go. Without action, nothing matters.

My panic attack was a wake-up call. I felt scared, and I'm not going to lie or sugarcoat it. I had no idea if I'd ever be able to speak again in public. For a couple of years, I struggled, but I never stopped. I kept taking action.

Besides Toastmasters, I pursued counseling. In the process, I found a therapist who helped me. All this struggle caused collateral damage and my marriage suffered. My wife, Michelle, was a rockstar during this time, coming to counseling too.

God certainly played a vital role. For the first time in my life, I looked up rather than merely looking forward. It's about putting in the work and believing in a higher power. Not either/or, rather both/and.

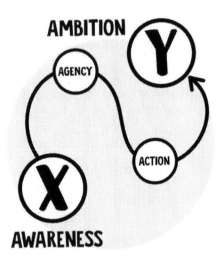

Today I take every opportunity when I'm invited to speak. I talk to sports teams, companies, internal teams, and clients. There's still a piece of me that's afraid I'll stumble. But I'm comfortable taking action despite the fear—and where I come from, that's the definition of courage.

On that topic, I want to encourage you today, and I want to build courage in you. Take action. Despite your challenges, take action. Your job is to move one step closer to your potential—to your ambition.

As I mentioned in my CORE above, my late friend, Scott Dinsmore, used to say we overestimate how much we can get done in a day, but we underestimate how much we can get done in a year. This book is a testament to that truth. I started writing it well over a year ago, and I only have a few weeks left before my deadline. Little by little, day by day, I've written and edited thousands and thousands of words. It's not an easy process. I've missed days and weeks, but I'm not quitting. I'm showing up so I can serve you because you're worth it.

Habits and Actions

At Northstar café in Columbus, Ohio, back in 2017, I sat with my friend James. We'd first met back in 2012 at the World Domination Summit. Our mutual friend Scott introduced us at that event in Portland. We spoke in a park at one of the nightly events. I knew there was something special about James. In his mid-twenties at the time, he had a quiet confidence that accompanied his humble aura. We had some things in common—both from Ohio. He went to college at Denison University, just down the street from where I lived. We traded numbers and stayed in touch.

Fast forward five years, and in-between bites we caught up on life. The restaurant popped with noise and people, packed with the rush. James shared about his struggle, trying to finish his first book. A couple of years back he'd signed a book deal, but on this day the grind got the best of him. He'd missed another deadline.

About a year later he finally published his book. Maybe you've heard of it—*Atomic Habits*.

At this present moment, it's still #1 on the *New York Times* bestseller list—selling over 10 million copies worldwide. The fact that James Clear struggled to get this book finished is something we can all take great comfort in.

He almost gave up. But he didn't. Doing great work isn't always a clean process. It's gritty, difficult, and messy.

I've interviewed James a couple of times on my podcast, and one of the key things he always talks about is environment design and the compound interest of work.

To finish *Atomic Habits*, James had to get creative. He'd leave his phone in another room. He deleted all social media from his phone. He took this to another level when he had his assistant, Lindsay, change his passwords so he couldn't get into these apps even if he tried. He took ruthless action to achieve his goal.

By showing up day after day, he eventually produced a masterpiece. James talks about the "aggregation of marginal gains" in *Atomic Habits*. He embodied this as he fought his way through the process. The real key to his success, though, was based on taking action consistently many years before.

In 2012 he started writing about habits and published an article every Monday and Thursday. He did this for a few years straight, never missing a deadline. He'll be the first one to tell you that every article wasn't great.

But he was consistent. He showed up and did the work. It resonated. He brought valuable content to the world. He has a knack for simplifying complex topics. *Atomic Habits* is #1 in the world for a reason. And James remains humble and grounded and, no doubt, he'll keep doing great work for years to come.

The Power of 1% Better Every Day

I embraced this mindset of "aggregation of marginal gains" and focused on small things done over time consistently. It was perfect timing for a guy like me, meeting someone like James back in 2012 and becoming a student of his work. As I was rebuilding my speaking skills, I embraced this "1% better every day" mindset. Going to Toastmasters each week was a good start. Figuring out ways to add value every day at work with my team and our clients was the next iteration of this. With each presentation and my focus on delivering value in every interaction, I saw my work paying off.

I was fortunate to get my career back on track. I even earned our Chairman's Club award for the top-performing rep a couple of years in a row. Settling wasn't an option. I knew I couldn't get complacent.

I reached out to some of the top performers in the company to get their advice on how I could keep improving and to learn from them. During a conversation with my colleague Scott, he asked me if I could do a read-out on what I was learning for our entire division. That conversation was in November and the division meeting was in January. I said yes, and I was on the hook to present.

Those three initial conversations turned into about twenty-five others. I named the project "success habits." I was in full-blown learning mode. My goal was to distill the best practices of our team and provide a meaningful read-out for the group at the January meeting. It was a labor of love—at least one hundred hours of work over sixty days. It culminated in me presenting to our division.

Remember the story of me bonking out with a panic attack? This was the same group I'd been speaking to back then. So, a few years after I had the biggest failure of my professional career, I was back on the same stage pouring into our team.

I was a different person.

I had done the work in the unseen hours to get back there. I don't say this to brag. There's nothing glorious about doing the reps. Rather, I share it to give you hope and inspiration. If a guy like me who literally couldn't speak in front of groups could figure out a way to rebuild from scratch, I promise you, you can do amazing things.

It centers on habits. See, I'm not sure you ever master a habit. Can you get good at something? Of course. Malcolm Gladwell proved this point well in *Outliers* with his retelling of Anders Ericsson's "10,000 Hour Rule." Invest the time with deliberate practice and you should attain mastery.

The more I've studied, the more I believe building a good habit and getting rid of a bad habit is a lifelong journey.

This is good news. It means what you do today is important. Taking action today is the most important thing. The image below depicts James Clear's take on identity-based habits.

Most people think in terms of outcome rather than identity, for example, *I want to lose ten pounds* vs. *I'm the type of person who works out.*

Notice the difference, in the words of James Clear: "The root of behavior change and building better habits is your identity. Each action you perform is driven by the fundamental belief that it is possible. So if you change your identity (the type of person you believe you are), then it's easier to change your actions."[9]

This is a complete flip from what we're traditionally taught about goals and habits. The goal is to show up today and do the work. Then show up again tomorrow. That's identity. That's becoming the person you want to be.

It's all about right now. Today!

I used to refer to myself as an "aspiring" writer. I started my first blog in 2009. I had wanted to write and publish a book since I was young. This is due in large part to my mom, an English teacher.

I never believed I would be a writer until someday in the future—the day I would be officially published. I think differently now. Anytime I write, I'm a writer. By the way, something like 80 percent of people in the world want to write a book. Most don't. All should. You're a writer if you start writing.

There's some research out there that says it takes sixty-six days to form a habit. Other research says seventeen days. I call BS on all of it. I know it takes a lifetime. There's a reason alcoholics fight every day to stay sober and continue to go to meetings. This stuff isn't easy. We need to be honest.

I don't know about you, but I love food. I grew up in a big Italian family, and pizza, pasta, and bread were staples. So were yummy Italian cookies. I eat pretty clean most of the time, but I still love this stuff. I have something of a reputation in my company for being the guy who never leaves a client dinner without ordering dessert. My mouth is watering as I'm typing this. (Make sure you try the chocolate peanut butter pie at Ocean Club if you ever visit Columbus, Ohio.)

I know this about myself. I know I like to indulge in dessert when I go out to eat. This means I have to work hard to eat as clean as possible at other times. I'm not always successful, but I'll assure you it's an area where I live with intention. Because of this commitment, I experience victory much of the time.

The STAR Formula

If you want to get closer to mastery in anything, you need to gain an understanding of how your environment impacts your thoughts and emotions. At the end of the day, you must determine what you're after.

A result? A feeling? A win?

The answer is different for everyone.

Here's what I know. Everything has a stimulus. Sometimes it's known (conscious), and sometimes it's unknown (subconscious). Regardless, the stimulus leads to a thought or feeling. This in turn leads you to an action (or inaction) that produces a result or outcome.

I call this the STAR Formula.

S = Stimulus

T = Thought/Emotion

A = Action (or Inaction)

R = Result

The key moment of truth is the space between your thoughts/emotions and your action. Knowing and mastering this is the key to good habit formation and bad habit reduction. Let's unpack it further.

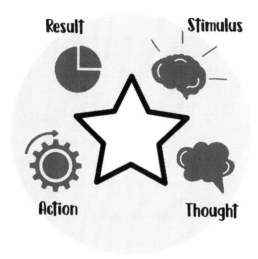

Stimulus

Stimuli are all around us. Your ability to gain awareness and understanding when it comes to these stimuli is a vital part of any behavior change. Some stimuli are good, and some are bad. If you're trying to curb alcohol consumption or battle sugar cravings, it's not a good idea to have beer front and center in the fridge or a box of Twinkies in the cupboard. Simply opening the fridge or the cabinet is the stimulus that leads to a thought or an action. Too many of these stimuli and it's difficult to resist temptation.

Good stimuli work in your favor. My wife is a clean eater, and we always have a fridge stocked with apples and a bowl on our kitchen island with oranges and avocados. So, I tend to eat more apples, oranges and avocados these days.

Thought/Emotion:

The stimuli you experience always lead to thoughts and emotions. Many times, a stimulus is subconscious. Your ability to understand the stimuli as well as the thoughts and emotions that accompany them is a crucial step toward success. This ties into awareness— the first step in the With Intention Wheel. This leads to the most important piece—taking action.

Action (or Inaction)

Action and inaction are both choices. They flow from our thoughts and emotions.

The key is to take productive action regardless of feelings.

"The heaviest weight at the gym is the front door." That's what former boxer Ed Latimore says.

We've all had the experience where we don't want to work out but push through anyway. Sometimes we break a sweat and enjoy an incredible workout. We release endorphins and punch Resistance in the face. Our productive action creates new thoughts and emotions. You can do this in any situation when you're in tune with your thoughts and emotions.

Results

When we take action, we produce results. Take enough productive action and you'll create remarkable and sustainable results. On the flip side, if you don't take enough action, your results will suffer. Your results are an accumulation of this process over time.

* * *

Caleb Porter, a former teammate, is one of our country's top soccer coaches. He's won two Major League Soccer championships in the last seven years—one with the Portland Timbers and one with the Columbus Crew. He's one of the fiercest competitors I ever played against, and he brings that tenacity to coaching.

The Crew won the MLS Cup in 2020. It was in the middle of the COVID-19 pandemic, so the season was thrown off course—to put it mildly. The teams played in stadiums that were only at 20 percent capacity.

During the MLS Cup championship game, Darlington Nagbe and Pedro Santos—two of the Crew's key starters—couldn't play. So the Crew started a rookie, Aidan Morris. In that game, he was arguably the most impactful player, helping them beat the Seattle Sounders 3–0 to win the title.

It's a wonder how you win a title without two of your key players, however, a video of Coach Porter talking to his team in the preseason about eight months earlier gives a clue. The team gathered around the coach to hear a powerful truth:

"Your daily discipline determines your destination."

Embodying this truth made the difference and helped them secure the championship. These Four Ds became a foundation for their title-winning season: *Daily Discipline Determines Destination.*

The best of the best remain steadfast when adversity strikes. Daily actions keep us moving forward even when we don't see an immediate reward, such as when a soccer season is hijacked by a pandemic.

Delayed Gratification

In 1972, a Stanford University professor, Walter Mischel, conducted an experiment famously referred to as the Marshmallow Test. Maybe you know the premise? The experiment measured the ability of children to delay immediate gratification.

The test was simple. Each child could have one marshmallow now or wait a little while and get two marshmallows.

Mischel then followed these kids for the remainder of their lives. He discovered that those who waited experienced more success later on in life. The researchers measured things like SAT scores, body mass index, and educational achievements.

All of these metrics take time, discipline, and action. We all have a gap between where we are and where we want to go—the gap between our X and our Y.

* * *

Elites embrace this gap. They're not discouraged or dismayed by it. Rather, they're motivated and inspired. They lean into this gap, and through daily discipline and delayed gratification, they close it.

A video of Drew Brees surfaced in recent years. A practice session ended and everyone left the building. But Drew kept going through simulated reps. All alone. Just Brees—his mind on fire—rehearsing, reviewing.

Reggie Bush, a Heisman Trophy winner and former teammate of Brees, captured the video. You should check it out, but here's what Bush said in those three minutes:

> A lot of people in this world want to be great. A lot of young guys talk about it . . . they want to be flashy . . . a lot of young guys want

the quick easy shortcut route to greatness. Ain't no shortcuts to greatness, man, this is what it's about right here. . . . About forty minutes now after practice, after a walk-through . . . and there's only one man out here on this field. Only one man going through the motions, getting his mental reps. How important are these mental reps right now, man, for this game tomorrow night?

This is what the leader of an organization, of a football team, looks like. Right here. This is what it takes, man. A lot of guys want to be great. A lot of guys aren't willing to go the extra mile for the man next to you . . . a lot of people are not willing to go to the depths, to the point to where you got to be by yourself sometimes. . . . Sometimes you need that quietness, that peace, man, to just get your mind right.

The unseen hours. That's when the elite separate themselves from everyone else. How are your unseen hours going? Do the work. Prepare. It will pay off.

The video continues:

Visualization is so important. Visualizing . . . what you want to do in a game. It doesn't even got to be sports, man, just visualizing the things that you're gonna do, going through the motions and the mental reps—this is what it takes. This is what it's about. . . .

Nobody in here but one man. Getting his mind right, doing what he needs to do to prepare himself for greatness—for tomorrow's game. And this is what he does *every week, every day*."[10]

83

The next week, Brees delivered a performance for the ages on Monday Night Football. He had twenty-nine completions on thirty attempts and threw for four touchdowns in a 34–7 win over the Colts. He also broke Peyton Manning's career record with his 540th touchdown pass.

An accident? Hardly.

> Brees was all but forgotten a few years into his career. Battling a shoulder injury, the Chargers no longer wanted him. . The Dolphins (and Nick Saban) famously passed on him. The New Orleans Saints and coach Sean Payton took a shot on Brees not long after Hurricane Katrina ravaged the city of New Orleans.

The unseen hours: our preparation, our practice. These are the difference makers that make the elites what they are—people and players who work and live with intention.

The Power of the Bamboo

My son, Gabe, often plays basketball at a local place called Just Hoops. There are a bunch of baskets, and we rent space and fire shots for an hour or so. They keep track of your baskets, and it's a great environment to get reps.

Recently, I saw a sign on their wall that resonated with me: "If you water giant timber bamboo in the first year, nothing happens. If you water the second year, nothing happens. If you water the third year, nothing happens. But when you water the bamboo the fourth year, it will rocket up an astonishing ninety feet in only sixty days."

If you're struggling with not getting the results you want, think about this bamboo analogy. This goes hand in hand with focusing on the labor and not the fruit. Figure out what your process is and win the day. Keep showing up. Over time, good things will happen. It may take longer than you think, but if you trust the process and are doing your "work" the right way, it's only a matter of time until you see results.

Every day brings you one step closer to your outcome. Easier said than done? Of course! Always simple. Never easy.

Divide and Conquer

When you're thinking about the required action ahead, it's easy to get overwhelmed. Each detail can feel like a mental mountain.

It reminds me of an interaction I had with my son the other day. While helping Gabe with his homework, I shared a lesson I'd learned twenty-nine years ago when I was a freshman at St. Edward High School in Cleveland. My English teacher, Brother Joe, taught us a concept he called "divide and conquer." I've often come back to his example.

In ninth grade, the work started piling up: reading books, writing papers, studying for tests. Brother Joe gave us some advice. Instead of doing it all in one sitting, we could divide it up and conquer each assignment one by one. It worked. By breaking it up, I felt a sense of satisfaction, and I found the momentum to complete the next task.

My wife, Michelle, was a second-grade schoolteacher for many years. She used to teach a concept called "micro-movements." Same idea.

An often-used analogy for productivity is eating an elephant. How do you do it? One bite at a time. I'm still not sure how or why you'd eat an elephant, but the point is that an elephant is big, and you can't "eat it" all at once, only one bite at a time.

Back in high school, my feelings of overwhelm faded as I completed each micro-session. In the process, I gained grit—a quality popularized by Angela Duckworth. This psychologist, former consultant, and college professor often observes people. Her research reveals "grit" as the defining characteristic of the most successful people. These resilient outliers viewed obstacles as opportunities, embodying a mindset that overcomes and performs despite challenges.[11]

Grit means coming back and doing it all over again the next day. Everyone falls, but only the gritty get back up.

Talent gets you in the game, but it doesn't keep you there. Talent must be mixed with effort. This combination produces skill. Grit takes awareness. Grit takes intention. Grit takes deliberate practice.

I don't think we're born with grit. Rather, we build it over time. And to do so, we must get comfortable with being uncomfortable.

Adjustment (I improve.)—Forever evolve so you contribute to your world in a meaningful way.

My dad went to heaven in 2018. He battled dementia for a few years and ended up in an assisted living facility for the last year and a half or so of his life. When I would visit him, I'd walk into the facility, check in, and head back to see him. Usually his girlfriend Sue was with him at the table feeding him his lunch.

My dad couldn't talk—at least not with his mouth. His eyes could talk though. He had these big brown eyes, and when he'd see me, they'd get even bigger. He'd push his tray of food away, hands shaking from the Parkinson's disease that had hijacked his body.

Slowly, he'd stand up. His mouth would move as though he wanted to say something, but no sound came out. The words came from his eyes. He saw me. He knew me.

I had the opportunity to be with him for his last breath. My brother called me early one morning and said, "Jon, you'd better get up here." I live in Columbus, which is about two hours from where my dad was, near Cleveland. I entered his room. He labored to breathe. His eyes closed, and I knew the end was near.

After a few hours, I could tell that everyone in my family was exhausted. At about 9 p.m., I insisted my brother, his wife, and Dad's girlfriend go home for the night to get some rest. I said I'd stay with him for a bit and then head over to one of their houses.

I played a worship song called "Oceans (Where Feet May Fail)" by the worship band Hillsong United. These lyrics are powerful, and they seemed fitting under the circumstances.

I prayed over him, and a few minutes later, he took his last breath. I was honored to be there.

When you experience the death of a loved one, emotions stir and memories surface. You plan the funeral and greet everyone as they pay their respects.

The memories still come to me in flashes.

One seems to stick and rise to the surface.

"Keep working. Keep getting better, Jon boy."

My parents instilled in me a mindset to continuously improve. I never understood the weight of those words until he passed away. And now as I live with intention, they mean more to me than I thought possible.

His words aren't only for me—except for the "Jon boy" part. We must all keep working and keep getting better. Adjustment is part of life because life is always changing. It's like a ship on the ocean; there's always movement.

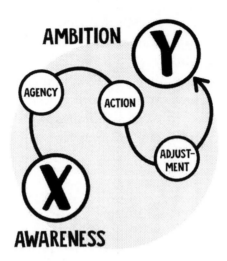

If everything were set in stone, there'd be no risk or growth. Change is one of the only constants in this life. The good thing about change is that it keeps things interesting. It also prevents us from becoming complacent. In sports, relationships, and business, complacency is the enemy of greatness.

If you're human, you've probably ordered something from Amazon. Amazon's motto through the years has been "Day 1." They realized the importance of never getting complacent early on and created a strategy to ensure victory. In fact, one of the main buildings at their headquarters is called Day 1. If you read any of their letters to shareholders, they always reference Day 1. Day 2 is called stasis, and stasis is complacency.

Daniel Slater, the worldwide lead for the culture of Amazon, unpacks this further in a blog post on their website:

> [Jeff] Bezos, in his 2016 Shareholder Letter, answered: "Day 2 is stasis. Followed by irrelevance. Followed by excruciating, painful decline. Followed by death. And that is why

it is always Day 1." To avoid Day 2 culture, a company must be hyper-vigilant, remain focused on its customers, and stave off practices that hamper its ability to rapidly innovate.

While we do not believe Amazon's approach is the only or best one, many of our customers ask us to share the lessons we've learned as we've grown, as well as some of the mechanisms we employ to ensure that it's always Day 1 at Amazon.[12]

The key is never to stop evolving and never to stop adjusting. I'm not saying you never rest or recover—these are essential to remaining in flow, the optimal state of human performance. Too many high performers shortcut rest and recovery, and they suffer as a result.

I am referring to constant growth. As we continuously improve and get better, we progress. I'm not delusional. I know some days it won't happen. But over time, by living With Intention, transformational days will add up. These days turn into months, the months into years, the years into decades, and—well you get the illustration.

An intentional life is a result of a bunch of intentional days strung together.

Here's how I keep the need for adjustment in front of me at all times. It's an exercise handed to me by my executive coach a few years back. He'd assign me videos to watch and content to read. My homework was simple—I had to write a response to what I saw and read. Two questions pulled the lessons right from my brain as long as I carved out the time to answer them sincerely:

1. What did I learn?
2. How do I apply?

"What did I learn?" caused me to look back and reflect.

"How do I apply" caused me to look forward and project.

These two questions became game-changers in my journey. They moved me from consumer to creator. They made me take action and adjust.

I encourage you to keep these two questions front and center for the remainder of this book. Ask yourself—

1. What did I learn?
2. How do I apply?

Kaizen

Toyota Motor Corporation is the largest auto manufacturer in the world. In 2008, they surpassed General Motors for the first time and haven't looked back. This didn't happen overnight.

One of the keys to Toyota's success is a focus on constant and never-ending improvement, otherwise known as *kaizen*. The people at Toyota are keen observers of their own processes and everyone else's. They study themselves and what others are doing.

In 1933, Toyoda Kiichiro founded the company as a subsidiary of his father's company, Toyota Automatic Loom Works. In 1950, a team from Toyota came to the United States to learn from the American manufacturers. After World War II, they'd ceased production and were on the brink of bankruptcy. They came to learn what was working. On their visit, they saw a lot of gaps and inefficiencies in the American process of vehicle production. The team came back to Japan inspired to get better and started to implement some of their discoveries. Soon after, they launched Toyota Sales USA and had their first big hit with the Toyota Corolla. The rest is history.

Toyota made it their passion to produce cars with intention. In fact, they followed the With Intention Wheel with precision. Notice the five components they applied:

CHAPTER 5

BUILD INTO OTHERS (I CAN)

*Before you build into people,
you must first value people.*

You, my brothers and sisters, were called to be free.
But do not use your freedom to indulge the flesh;
rather, serve one another humbly in love.
—The Apostle Paul, to the Church at Galatia

Thus far it's been all about you. And it should be.
Remember, "Love your neighbor *as yourself.*"
And "In the event of an emergency, put on your
oxygen mask first before helping someone else."

The time comes, however, when we take our eyes off
ourselves and build into others. After all, what's the point
of getting better if it's only benefiting us personally? Living
with intention starts with us, then flows into others, and
then flows back into us.

The cycle continues, never ceasing. It's not supposed to end.
Congruence. Permanence. Transcendence.

Jon Gordon, one of my favorite authors and speakers, often talks about shifting from a "me" to a "we" mindset. There's power in serving others and contributing in a meaningful way.

Now when I speak, I don't take it for granted. My perspective shifted from "How do I sound?" to "How can I give?" I still have fears, but I trust the work, and I prepare as best I can. It's my passion to give to others. I've also adopted this approach in my professional career. I no longer sell or focus on making my quota. Rather, I put the customer first. When my focus changed, so did my results. I've experienced new levels of success, and in the process, I've been positioned to lead a team. My goal is now to help my team improve and grow.

It's ironic. As we grow ourselves, our influence grows. We shift from success to significance.

The With Intention Wheel also shifts from a "me" focus to a "we" focus. Along the way, we pick up five new capabilities:

1. Sincerity
2. Empathy
3. Resourcefulness

4. Value
5. Energy

With Intention Wheel - Others

In the rest of this chapter, we'll unpack each one.

Sincerity (I can be honest.)—Serve others authentically so you can build trust and rapport.

These days being authentic is on the rise, and for good reason. It pops out because it's so rare. Social media made us skeptical. We can spot a fake easier than ever. Many people put up a front or a filter. They pretend to be someone they're not.

Reflect upon your last week. Think about five people you've interacted with in work or life, personally or professionally. On a scale of one to ten, how sincere were those interactions? Many of those conversations may have lacked sincerity.

Especially today, people crave true interaction. We've all been through a lot in recent years: sickness, war, shutdowns, recessions. Authentic connections surpass these setbacks.

Want to build trust? Open up. Show vulnerability. Confide in others. Serve people.

Here are three actions that make a major difference:

1. **Tell Your Story**: When I modeled transparency about my challenges, connections deepened and relationships strengthened. Others followed my lead and opened up about their challenges. They came to me for advice and mentorship, and I gladly provided it. I don't have all the answers, but I've battled through challenges and learned many lessons along the way. Share what's worked for you and what hasn't worked for you. The fact you share both makes you more valuable to others. This vulnerability builds trust. That opens the door to greater levels of influence.

2. **Work Together to Find a Solution**: I've found in business and life that the best solutions typically come from collaboration, especially when negotiating a contract. I'm not a big fan of putting a deal together on paper and forcing it on someone. This becomes a tug of war and often leads to someone feeling they "won" and someone feeling they "lost." I'd rather have everyone walk away feeling great about the situation.

3. **Think Transformational, Not Transactional**: Short-term thinking is a recipe for disaster. When dealing with anyone—an individual or an organization—always think about the long-term implications. Sometimes you have to take a short-term loss for a

to stop.

long-term win. This is the path to true victory and true sincerity.

Empathy (I can empathize.)—Listen with your heart and help others feel heard.

When I first took over my team in 2017, I reached out to some trusted friends and advisors. I asked my friend Shawn, the CFO of a large international company, what he thought his key to leadership was. I expected a complex answer. I thought he'd mention financials, but they never came up.

He told me the key was all about the heart and how you make people feel. He said if people know how much you care about them, they will move mountains for you. Commitment flows from care. I've never forgotten his answer, and it shapes me as a leader to this day.

Empathy is the ability to think from someone else's perspective. Understanding their feelings is much easier said than done. Humans are inherently selfish, and we gravitate toward our perspective first and foremost; however, being more empathetic does wonders for you and the people you lead.

I've learned empathy as a result of adversity. The greater the challenges I face, the more empathetic I become. When we face difficult circumstances, it gives us perspective.

When people around me need empathy, I try to take three actions:

1. **Seek to Understand**: People want to feel heard. It's one of our core needs. In *The 7 Habits of Highly Effective People*, Steven Covey exhorts us to "seek first to understand, then to be understood."[13] Although we want to

get our point across and do the talking, if we step back and listen, we will learn empathy on a whole new level.

2. **Go Deeper**: I refer to transformational relationships as "layer-three" relationships. These types go well below the surface. When we "peel back the onion," our ability to build trust grows exponentially. Layer-one relationships stick to the facts. Layer-two relationships focus on a person's likes or dislikes. But layer-three relationships discover what makes people tick—their true feelings and authentic purpose.

3. **Follow Up**: Checking in on someone and following up demonstrates concern. Even a simple text message a few days after a conversation makes you an outlier. One of my favorite follow-ups is three simple words: *tell me more*. When you invite someone to share their heart, you'll be surprised how far they let you in.

My friend and colleague Shep often says, "Be interested, not interesting." When we're interested more than interesting, we're headed in the right direction.

Resourcefulness (I can produce.)—Determine how to get the job done, even when times are tough.

Thinking outside the box is a great skill to have. Sometimes the answers aren't in front of us, and we must be innovative and creative to get the job done.

There's a time to get gritty—to get outside ourselves. Excuses are easy to find. Most people will reach out and cling to one as the rationale for giving up. But your ability to overcome challenges and find solutions sets you apart.

My friend Kary Oberbrunner says, "Your *defying* moment becomes your *defining* moment."

In the process, you become indispensable— winning in the good times and the bad ones.

The COVID-19 pandemic is all the evidence you need. Most businesses struggled. Many folded and ceased to exist. Some reinvented themselves, tapped into a new type of resourcefulness, and gained market share.

Our business, like many other businesses, confronted this reality. Would we step up, or would we pack it in? Our team made successful strides, controlling what was in our power to control. We kept producing and creating value for our clients, and they noticed.

Pandemic or not, there will always be challenges in every environment. Your ability to overcome these challenges by getting the job done in tough times will separate you from the pack. It's inevitable.

Take a peek at history and you'll see all the proof you need; you'll find so many great examples of resourcefulness.

- Nelson Mandela remained in prison for twenty-seven years. Nevertheless, he still found a way to stay purpose-driven, eventually leading the country that imprisoned him.
- Helen Keller was deaf and blind and still redefined the way we view people with disabilities.
- Winston Churchill successfully led Great Britain through World War II despite extreme odds.

- Abraham Lincoln overcame multiple defeats and chronic depression to become one of the greatest US Presidents.

- Corrie Ten Boom's family hid Jewish people during the Holocaust. She was eventually arrested and put in a concentration camp, then released, without letting bitterness destroy her. She forgave the people who tortured her and killed her sister. Her family was credited with saving approximately eight hundred lives.

The moral of these stories is simple: There's always a way to remain resourceful. You have to keep working to find it.

I recommend focusing on three actions to remain resourceful:

1. **Control the Controllables**: There are always things within your control. These are things you can influence. If you worry about things outside of your control, you'll get overwhelmed. Focus on what you can control today.

2. **Be Proactive**: Do the work. Once you've identified what you can control (your attitude, your mindset, your actions), take a step toward that, even if it's a small step. Small steps over time lead to big things. (Remember the bamboo story from earlier.)

3. **Use Your Imagination**: Get creative. Go for a walk or a run and just think. Do some writing and get courageous. Don't be afraid to seek advice as well. Some of the best ideas for solving problems can come from a trusted advisor who is not "caught up in the weeds." This fresh perspective might be exactly what you need.

Value (I can provide.)—Deliver value in every interaction so you will be relied upon.

Some people struggle to build relationships and maintain friendships. I don't. I love people, and socializing comes easy for me. When I unpack this capability, it all centers on consistently delivering value.

In business and life, it's easy to get your foot in the door; however, unless you're adding value, that door will eventually shut. Once I learned how to leverage trust to keep building and serving, everything changed for the better. I describe it like this: trust + value = transformational partnerships.

Simple to understand yet difficult to do—like many principles from this book. This is why many people settle for transactional relationships that produce mediocre results.

When we listen with intention, we discover opportunities to serve and add value. It's the little things that make the difference: showing care, staying curious, asking questions, articulating, whiteboarding, visioning, discussing, and at times debating.

It's a flywheel.

For me, it starts with curiosity—often in the form of a whiteboard session. The whiteboard helps us all create a visual picture we can expand upon. After our time together, we'll take a picture of our whiteboard. This memorializes the experience. Then we can go back to it.

We build immense trust by adding value. And good things happen. I've learned from my experience in the business world that "happy customers buy more stuff." Sales come, but sales are never the driver here. That's the lagging indicator. The score takes care of itself.

Energy (I can keep up.)—Bring positive energy to your relationships and interactions.

We all have two energies—the energy we use to fuel ourselves and the energy we use to fuel others. They are interdependent. We'll struggle to fuel others when we're empty. And when we're full of energy, we can't help but fuel others.

A few years back, I heard my friend Alan Stein Jr. share a story that illustrates this point. He spoke to our company about Steve Nash, a two-time NBA MVP. Although Nash is now the coach of the Brooklyn Nets, back when he played, he was an undersized guard. Most colleges passed on him, and he ended up at Santa Clara (a mid-major school). He was drafted in the fifteenth round in 1996 by the Phoenix Suns. He didn't have much of an impact early in his career. After a couple of seasons, he was traded to the Dallas Mavericks and eventually became an All-Star there, then re-signed with the Suns where he won his MVPs.

Nash was a fantastic shooter, but he had two superstar qualities that made him a rare gem. He excelled as a passer—the assist guy. If you watch footage of him playing, you'll see his main focus was setting up his teammates. He gave them the ball in places where they could score. This made him a popular teammate, and others loved playing with him.

But here's the more important piece. Nash was an energizer. He was determined to bring positive energy to the game and his teammates. An intern for the Suns once tracked the number of high fives and fist bumps Nash gave his teammates on game day. Want to guess what the number was?

239!

Nash gave his teammates a positive touch 239 times. Each one infused energy into his teammates, building trust and positive connections. With every fist bump, slap on the back, and high five, Nash solidified his winning status.

Dean Smith, the late, great coach of the University of North Carolina, used to coach his team not to celebrate themselves after they scored. They instead celebrated the teammate who passed them the ball with either a high five (if they were close) or they pointed at the teammate in a gesture of gratitude.

These touches matter—physical touches or metaphorical ones. A quick text to let someone know you're thinking about them or even making eye contact can create powerful connections.

Don't underestimate the power you have to lift up someone else. The more you bring energy to others, the better you'll feel. As a result, your energy will increase.

We've brought this truth into our work environment by creating what I like to call a "high-five culture." We intentionally recognize people when they do good work. Our 250 employees represent account managers, customer success managers, consultants, field service reps, and other key personnel who serve our clients. Every other month we conduct market calls. The highlight of every call is the recognition piece.

Leaders each take turns recognizing employees for high performance. People are nominated by their peers and honored by name. Although it's a little thing, it's not so little. Much like Steve Nash's 239 touches, creating this "high-five" culture builds trust and connection.

We also recognize every work anniversary and birthday. This leads to countless email exchanges and oftentimes funny pictures and loving jesting. Each one is a mini high five and serves as fuel for greater connection and trust.

If you lead anything—including your family— reflect upon how intentional you are with creating a high-five culture. Can you high-five more people? Can you step up how you recognize others? Think about the type of energy you bring into relationships. Could you improve? If so, how?

A few years ago, our family improved in this area by reading and applying a book. I highly recommend *How Full is Your Bucket? For Kids* by Tom Rath. This children's book, adapted from an adult book, is simple but powerful.

The author asks readers to imagine everyone they encounter having a bucket on top of their head with some water in it. Everybody has two jobs. The first is not to do or say something that spills water out of the bucket. The second job is to fill the bucket with water.

Simply put, the author asks us to consider if we're bringing positive or negative energy to our interactions with people. We often overcomplicate this principle. Bottom line, be someone who fills buckets rather than empties them.

John Gottman and his wife Julie study successful relationships. In their research of couples, they've found that to have an enduring relationship the positive interactions need to outweigh the negative. They even identified the magic number. Successful relationships have five positive interactions for every one negative interaction—5:1.

You might think that's pretty hard to do. I agree. But this is where the intentionality comes in. To make any relationship thrive, you must focus on positive, encouraging interactions that build connection, trust, and rapport. This stored relational equity helps when the friction comes. All this positivity lubricates the friction and helps both parties to push through and maintain the good vibes.

A few years ago, I spoke to the soccer team at my alma mater, Bowling Green State University. Before my speech, I watched their training session. I realized how times have changed over the past twenty years.

The team placed a high priority on energy and peak performance, as evidenced by the fact that every player wore a heart rate monitor. The coaches had an app on their iPads where they tracked the work rate of each player and their overall energy level. They assessed how long players should train. All this data helped them make on-the-spot decisions about pushing the intensity or dialing it back. They monitored this "threshold score" carefully, not overstepping it.

I chuckled to myself, fully aware of the lack of this technology back when I'd played. Our coaches were notorious for grinding us down. They implemented two- or three-hour training sessions from time to time if we weren't producing. Although this built grit, I'm not sure it was the best for sustaining optimal performance.

All of my research on productivity demonstrates the need for intentional energy management. Time is finite after all. We all get the same twenty-four hours in a day, and a focus on restoring energy produces helpful outcomes.

Here are my top eight tips to optimize your energy and performance:

1. **Sleep**: Get great sleep—eight hours a night, ideally. Going to bed earlier has a big impact on your energy for the next day.

2. **Exercise**: Increase your heart rate at least four days a week. Breaking a sweat daily is even better, even if only on a walk outside. This delivers a psychological benefit as well as a physical benefit.

3. **Rest:** Take consistent breaks throughout your day. Get up and walk around. Especially in today's work environment with so many virtual calls, it's vital to oscillate between your work and rest.

4. **Margin:** Schedule margin. Don't overbook yourself with meetings and calls. Doing so dumps cortisol into your bloodstream, unleashing an abundance of byproducts that negatively impact your health. Don't be afraid to block "margin" time on your calendar.

5. **Breathing:** A regimen of deep breathing does wonders. There are many methods, but I suggest a 5-20-5 method for starters. Breathe in for 5 seconds. Hold your breath for 20 seconds. Breathe out for 5 seconds. Repeating this one or two times brings more energy, calm, and peace.

6. **Electronics:** Put away your phone at times throughout the day. Physically removing it from your presence is best as studies show "phantom" notifications are a real thing. I get that this isn't easy if you're in a customer-facing role. Do what you can to be intentional about not looking at your phone or computer screen every moment of the day.

7. **Journal:** Get curious. Write down your thoughts. Besides helping you process, reflect, and become more self-aware, journaling also archives your best thinking—allowing you to revisit personal and professional breakthroughs. Physical journals are best. Electronic ones can perpetuate distractions.

8. **Intentionality:** Since you're reading a book called *With Intention*—of course you know you need to integrate intentionality throughout your day. Make

a conscious choice to start your day with purpose. For me, investing a little time reading the Bible centers me and gets me pointed in the right direction. Purpose and spiritual connection keep you energized throughout the day.

PART 3
THE PINNACLE
The Outcomes of With Intention

CHAPTER 6

THE OUTCOMES OF WITH INTENTION (I AM)

Living with intention is the surest way to leave a lasting legacy.

Show up filled up.
—Kary Oberbrunner

Build yourself. Serve others. That's the premise of this book. Be intentional about both. One without the other is no good.

Our world is in desperate need of people who live with intention.

Gallup's latest polling shows that four in ten adults world-wide experienced a lot of worry or stress. The COVID 19 pandemic hasn't helped as the prevalence of anxiety and depression has increased by 25%. More than 37 million Americans take antidepressants. I believe in taking medicine for the right reasons, and who am I to judge what those right reasons are? That said, I believe the number of people living without intention is higher now than ever before in human history. Guess what? I think these two statistics are linked—those on antidepressants and those living without intention.

As we've seen throughout this book, intention deficit disorder is real. Pictures are often helpful to put this into perspective. Many of us are visual learners after all. Notice the Intention Focus Matrix© below.

Let's unpack this matrix, one quadrant at a time:

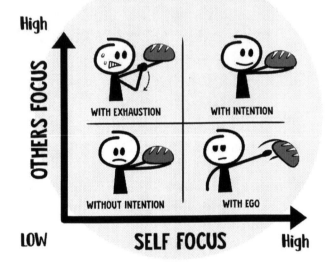

- **Quadrant 1: With Exhaustion (High Others Focus | Low Self Focus)**—If you're focused too much on others and not enough on yourself, you burn out. While it's a noble thing to serve others, you can't neglect yourself in the process.
- **Quadrant 2: With Intention (High Others Focus | High Self Focus)**—Though some may debate it,

this is the best place to be. Because we take care of ourselves, we can also take care of others. Because we show up filled up when it comes to personal growth, we can pour value into other people.

- **Quadrant 3: Without Intention (Low Others Focus | Low Self Focus)**—This is when you don't focus on building yourself or others. Because you don't prioritize either, you slip into a bad state. Stay here too long and this is hazardous to your physical and mental health.

- **Quadrant 4: With Ego (Low Others Focus | High Self Focus)**—When we have an unhealthy fixation on ourselves to the detriment of others, we become egotistical. In this quadrant, we're the hero, the topic, and the focus. This selfish place is the precursor to many people's downfall.

Results (I am contributing.)

I feel as though I've been blessed to get a second chance in life, both personally and professionally.

Many years ago, I was at a breaking point, but by the grace of God, I've transformed. By working the With Intention Wheel, I experienced personal and professional success.

Was it easy?

Not on your life. Did it take time? Absolutely. But, looking back, I can tell you with 100 percent certainty that it was worth it.

I still have bad days. But at least now I know why those bad days happen. Wherever and whenever I live Without Intention, I set myself up for failure. I'm not immune to circumstances or emotions. But I've discovered and developed tools and tactics to combat these tendencies and temptations.

I know this for sure—if I can do it, then you can too. Maybe at this exact moment, you're experiencing incredible victory. Or maybe you're at your lowest place in life. Regardless, every challenge is an opportunity to learn and grow. Sometimes the best action we can take is to get our eyes off of ourselves.

As I was finding my footing again in the business & speaking world, I jumped at the opportunity to co-lead those mission trips. Although I knew my weaknesses, insecurities, and struggles, I dove in and made it a point to give what little I felt I had. Here's the crazy thing—when I did, I received back a hundredfold. Besides affirmation and encouragement, I also gained confidence.

Serving with my family on those mission trips was one of the most important activities I've ever done. Seeing my wife and daughters paint the nails of refugee moms or my son kicking a soccer ball with a refugee child—these moments were nothing short of amazing. I teared up watching them serving others.

When we embody a contribution mindset rather than a consumer one, everything changes. This shift is intentional, not accidental. It's a result of being proactive, and it shapes our legacy. Consider these questions:

How can I add value to every interaction?

How can I listen more than I talk?

How can I help someone feel heard?

How can I move the needle and help someone get closer to their potential?

How can I put myself in the best position to serve others?

These simple but powerful questions propel you in the right direction. You can have all the success and make all the money in the world, but it doesn't matter if it's all self-focused. Over time, you'll resent it. We weren't created for ourselves but rather for others. Influencers who shift from success to significance experience true joy. Unleashing and unlocking results in others generates genuine fulfillment in us.

There's a famous saying attributed to many people, "You make a living by what you get and you make a life by what you give." What type of life are you making today?

Influence (I am important.)

False humility doesn't help anyone. Sure, pride leads to many people's downfall, but so does low self-esteem. When people walk around thinking little of themselves—consumed with how bad they are—they settle for taking, not giving. They're needy, obsessed with scarcity and lack.

Influencers who have healthy self-esteem walk around knowing they can create value. They're not needy. They're focused instead on giving, in tune with abundance.

The word "influencer" can create negative connotations. But influence is agnostic. We can influence people for good or evil, depending on what we're plugged into—greed and gain or generosity and giving.

Influencing means movement. It represents action and change. Maybe it's a big transformation, or maybe it's a subtle shift. Everyone has the ability and power to be a person of influence. And like the circle illustration from a few chapters ago, we can grow our influence.

Imagine you have a servant's heart. Imagine all the good you can create for others—and yourself. People are attracted to those committed to helping others.

Fulfillment (I am joyful.)

I've never met someone who doesn't want fulfillment. On our deathbeds, we all want to have lived well. In sports, we call this "leaving it all on the field." When competing, we want to feel good about the effort we gave. Some people call this "feeling worthy" or having the ability to look at yourself in the mirror and like the person looking back at you.

Everyone struggles—but many people don't like to show it. This is one reason to be careful about who you look up to or follow on social media. I prefer people who are real. They are authentic about the good stuff and the bad stuff. They are real and raw, but they stay grounded and positive through it all.

This is why I love the word *courageous*. It means strength in the face of pain or grief. Intentional living is courageous living—both for you and for others. Our call is to find the strength to inspire others to keep going. This is the very definition of encouragement—giving courage to others.

Last time I checked, the world is in desperate need of encouragement.

AFTERWORD

CRAFT YOUR
WITH INTENTION PLAN (WIP)

Your With Intention Plan is your best
weapon against intention deficit disorder.

One of my favorite movies growing up was *Raiders of the Lost Ark*. Harrison Ford played the main character, Indiana Jones—an archaeologist traveling the world in search of the long-lost Ark of the Covenant.

His primary weapon of choice was a whip. He wielded this whip to beat bad characters, navigate rough terrain, and cross treacherous snake-filled pits. It was his go-to tool to survive and thrive.

Over the years, I've developed a powerful process to help you craft your own WIP. (Since I'm the author, I chose to drop the letter *h* in the word *whip*. As an author, you can do things like this.)

If you put the acronym WIP into a search engine, you'll find it has several meanings. Firstly, WIP relates to each of us—Work In Progress. None of us have arrived, and hopefully, we'll never stop growing. Secondly, WIP relates to this book—With Intention Plan. Notice our journey thus far:

Part 1: The Problem—Intention Deficit Disorder

Part 2: The Path—With Intention

You've taken a deep dive into understanding the problem and the path. You've discovered the With Intention Wheel and the five components to help you create a life with intention.

Now I want to invite you to craft your personal plan: your WIP (With Intention Plan).

There comes a time when we must stop learning and start living. Indiana Jones seemed to think so. There are many powerful quotes from this character, but here's one of my favorites:

"You want to be a good archaeologist . . . you gotta to get out of the library!"[14]

When I started writing this book, I made a personal commitment to practice what I preach by pouring on the value and overdelivering. As a result, even though the book is about to end, our journey doesn't have to. This is why I'm inviting you to craft your WIP.

I've created a mini course to help you do this. As a reader, you have free access to this online experience. By taking three simple steps, you'll gain the clarity you need to craft your own With Intention Plan:

Step 1: Current State

Step 1: 2: Future State

Step 3: Close the Gap

I look forward to helping you take your next step.

—Jon

Discover Your With Intention Quotient™ (WIQ)

Take the Free Assessment

https://training.jongiganti.com/assessment

APPENDIX

ADDITIONAL LIST OF STANDARDS FROM MY CORE

- **Effective, not productive.** It's not about productivity or efficiency. I get the right stuff done. I have an awareness of the 20 percent that has the highest impact, and I focus on the productive actions that help me execute. I will tend toward being more "efficient" and "optimized," and I will resist the temptation to fall back into old habits and systems.

- **Focused on deep-seated, transformational relationships.** Although with a few, these relationships are filled with love and admiration. This provides fuel for me as I'm fueling and building into others. This is magic when it's reciprocal. This lights me up.

- **Humble and confident.** I check my ego and remain authentic and humble. At the same time, I believe in my ability to deliver value and love. When these two dance together, there is no limit to the impact I can have. Souls can be ignited by this combination.

- **Fueled for elite performance.** I fuel my mind, body, and soul like an Olympic athlete. There's no difference between an elite athlete/coach and an elite sales leader. I'm tuned in to my body and mind and know that the right food, drink, sleep, and energy enhancers are crucial for this level of performance.

- **Relentless.** My whole life I've been a fighter, and that will continue. I have a relentless desire to live, love, give, and serve others. Embrace this. It's uncommon.

- **A work in progress.** I understand this is a journey. There will be ups and downs. I will make mistakes and I will have "wins" along the way. Losses are simply opportunities to learn. Embrace them.

- **Chasing acute pain.** Chronic pain is no joke and a terrible way of being. This leads to misery. Acute pain is where you discover the magic. Stress and rest = growth.

- **Alive.** I'm alive at an unbelievable time. This is a gift. I'm living abundantly and purposefully. This doesn't mean I won't face setbacks, but I pinch myself with the ,awareness of the glory of life and breath.

- **Aware of the fragility of life.** At a moment's notice, life can change. Death, adversity, challenges—they're constant. We live in a broken world, and the realization of this is a gift. And it's also a beautiful world once you realize it's not perfect. Losing my mom and dad, as well friends like TJ and Scott, hurts. They taught me so much. I will honor them through my work and life.

- **Hopeful.** My faith, purpose, and commitment to serving and doing the hard work give me hope for the future. Regardless of circumstance, my hope is grounded in the present and the eternal.

- **Hard on self, not down on self.** I expect a lot of myself, and I maintain extreme belief in my abilities. Setbacks will happen, and it's about how I respond. It's this drive to excel that will keep me moving forward.

- **Decisive.** Think and act, but don't second guess. There are no perfect decisions. Imperfect action is better than the quagmire of overthinking.

- **Okay with tension.** I put the tension where it needs to be. This means embracing conflict when necessary. Honest and open conversations are crucial. If done the right way, they are transformative. It's not about the conflict. It's about ownership, learning, and moving forward. We're all a work in progress. We all have blind spots.

- **Resourceful.** There's typically a solution somewhere, and it's up to me to find it. I'm okay with my back against the wall. I embrace that. I pride myself on being a problem solver.

- **Comfortable being uncomfortable.** I embrace discomfort. I know good things happen when I'm uncomfortable, and I push through this. Things like speaking, leading small groups, and speaking up in meetings are all opportunities. I trust I've done the work and will prepare as needed to execute in the moment.

- **Focused on slowing down.** I am present and aware. While my mind may be pushing me to go faster, I push back and stay in the "awareness" zone. I breathe. I write. I listen. I am still. I walk without a destination. I love. I laugh. I play. I rest. I slow down to speed up . . . but the speed is intentional and on life- and energy-giving things.

- **Committed to intentional rest.** I know the importance of rest. I don't shortchange the needs of my mind, body, and soul. When I'm between the lines, I work diligently. Outside the lines, I rest. This recharges me and fuels my ability to deliver, impact others, and be present and fully alive.

- **Joyful.** John Piper talks about the joy we get from desiring God.[15] I love this. I find joy in the day-to-day and the mission that I'm on. I don't confuse joy with happiness or being stress-free. There will be tough days and tough times, but having a joy-driven foundation keeps me grounded and at peace with whatever comes in my path. Joyful = fulfilled.

- **Aware of my breathing.** We come out of the womb with the gift of breathing in and out. We aren't taught how. I'm deeply aware of my breaths and know when it's time to pause and reengage with my breathing. The parasympathetic or subconscious awareness zone is where I operate. Much like surface-level level-one thinking, surface-level breathing is only the start—a decent guide. But level-two breathing (again, like thinking and emotions) is big, deep, and slow—and where I'm at my best.

- **A day winner.** Today is the day. Win the days. As my late friend Scott Dinsmore used to say, "We overestimate what we can get done in a day, but we underestimate what we can get done in a year." When I win days consistently, it has a cumulative effect, much like compound interest.

- **A moment embracer.** Days are made of moments, and I'm keenly aware of the key moments of the day. I'm tuned in and ready to pounce when those moments arrive. Like a lion chasing down a gazelle, I have my eyes wide open, ears ready, and heart focused.

- **Loving wholehearted.** I love others. My family first, of course, but other people feel the love I have for them through how I talk, what I say, and how I make them feel. Love brings connection.

- **At peace.** I feel great about the journey I'm on and can rest in the fact that I'm making progress daily. And my belief in my Maker grants me peace, serenity, and grace.

- **Courageous.** The word *cor* in Latin means "of the heart." When I lead heart-first, great things can happen. Keep leaning in.

Acknowledgments

Writing a book is something I've always wanted to do but never thought it would become a reality. My goal with this book is to serve you, the reader, and add value to your life. I can't thank you enough for investing the time to read With Intention. My hope and prayer is that it's encouraged you and planted some seeds for you to be more intentional with your life.

I have been fortunate to learn from so many amazing people through the years and to actually finish this book over the last two years, I had to rely on so many people.

First and foremost, my wife Michelle, who has served as a reader, editor, psychologist, prayer warrior and, most importantly, an incredible mom to our three kiddos. There were many late nights and early mornings for me and many weekends where I was holed up in our basement or in my office, of some nook and cranny of a spot in our house. Thank you, Michelle, for being my rock during this time. My children - Gabe, Reese and Emerson - thank you for your encouragement and inspiration. Being a dad is the greatest gift I've ever received.

I've leaned on so many to help with the craft of writing and, frankly, to stay out of my own way as doubts crept in. I'd like to thank Kary Oberbrunner, who's been a trusted advisor and partner for many years and helped me immensely with crafting this message. I could not have done it without you, Kary. You're a true friend and brother! Lori Piotrowski, who was the project manager on this. Your words of wisdom have been so helpful during this process. Melissa Fultz, thank you for keeping me on track with illustrations and for all of your help crafting those. Rikki Milbrandt, thanks for helping to get this book across the finish line. And, big thanks to Abigail Young for your copy editing prowess and to the entire Ethos Collective and Igniting Souls Publishing team. There is no way this book gets completed without you all!

I stand on the shoulders of so many. I've always been fascinated with learning - whether it's reading books or seeing people speak or attending some type of training. I've been super fortunate to learn from some of the best of the best.

My parents were both teachers. My mom, Kitty - an English teacher, inspired me at an early age to read and write. I held off for a while on the writing piece mom, but I hope this book is a testament to all she invested in me. Although we lost her last year, I know she's been with me during this entire process and is smiling down from Heaven. My dad, Frank, always encouraged me to be the best I could be and to keep working. Dementia took him in 2018 way too early but I know he's up there as well smiling down.

I'm blessed to have many trusted advisors, encouragers and friends in my corner. A huge thanks to the following, who have helped in so many ways:

My big brothers, Mario and Sam - Even though I was the punk little brother for many years, you guys always pushed me to work hard, compete and get better. Our friendship now is something I deeply cherish.

Lynn and Darlene Kreuzer - To the best in-laws a guy could have ever wished for. Your faith, prayers and encouragement mean so much and your commitment to each other is so admirable.

Michael Port - For helping me launch an investigation and pushing me to be vulnerable. You were the catalyst for me to share my story in this detail. I'm forever grateful to you.

Alan Stein Jr. - For your encouragement through this entire process. Thanks for always being so positive and encouraging. You're a world-changer.

Danny Bader - For all of your wisdom, friendship and support. Thanks for always being available and for the wisdom you always provide.

Mike Williams - For giving me wise words and encouragement when I needed it during this process. You're one of the kindest souls I've ever met.

James Clear - Your work has inspired me greatly and it's been fun to watch your journey. Your sound advice through this process has been super helpful. The work you've put out into the world and the Atomic Habits approach has been a guiding light for me and there's no way I could've written this book without your teaching, inspiration and friendship.

All of my former soccer coaches & teammates - Thank you for building into me and being great teammates and friends (especially my coaches - Bob Munn, Bob Culler, Dennis Weyn, Rocco Valente, Sandor Jakab, Joe Raduka, Tony Niccoli, Gary Palmisano, Mel Mahler & Wade Jean). Too many teammates to name but I love you guys. The lessons learned on sports teams are some of the most profound we will ever learn.

Ray Briles - For your belief in me and for calling me out when I needed to be called out. Thank you for your friendship and trust. This message doesn't happen without your investment in me.

Barrett Callaghan - For your encouragement and giving me a second chance in my career and for showing me what an inspirational servant leader looks like.

Chris Shepherd - For your friendship & encouragement through this process and your commitment to your faith and leadership.

My CCC Sales team - Ryan Squire, Greg Merante, Seth Mullady, Erik Bundgard and Joe Sickles - you guys inspire me to be a better leader every day. Iron sharpens iron and I appreciate you guys so much. I consider you brothers and true friends.

Scott Janik & Jerod Willey - For pushing me to present my research in 2015 - that was the start of this entire With Intention project. You both are great examples of servant leaders.

The entire CCC team - I've had the opportunity to learn from some of the best and pay it forward by mentoring many people along the way. It's been an honor to be a part of such a great team for the last 23 years. What a ride it's been. Thank you, Githesh Ramamurthy, for leading the way.

Greg Rortvedt, Dominic Caruso, Michelle Raue, Kari Turner Davis, Roy Hall, Ali Nasser & Brian Glibkowski - Being able to interview you all has been a gift and I can't thank you enough for investing the time with me.

All of my past, present (and future :) clients - I've learned so much from all of you and you've taught me the importance of serving first and being relentless in delivering value to our partnerships.

Sam Vest - You taught me so much about the business early in my career and have been a friend and mentor ever since.

Edgar Meza - Thank you for your friendship and for waking me up many years ago. I needed a wake up call to ensure I was doing business the right way. I'm sorry it took me a while to catch up :)

Jose Frias, Edgar Fiol, and the entire Loya team - You gave me the chance to earn your trust and show the value of our partnership. The work we did together helped transform me into a value-first salesperson.

Debra Seminario & Bart Mazurek - The work we did together many years ago helped me realize the importance of a team approach. Serving our clients doesn't happen without a team.

The Friday morning men's group - It's the best and most important meeting we have every week.

David Milroy - For your friendship, prayers and helping me understand the power of faith.

The Smith NAPC Small Group - This group meant so much to Michelle and I as we were navigating our future. Thanks for pouring into us (especially Patrick & Erin Smith).

Mike & Karla Muzi - Leading small groups together was a blast and you helped Michelle and I lean into our faith. Thank you!

Andy Larned - For jumping in full throttle at 658 - leading with you was a blast and doing God's work together was nothing short of amazing.

Adam Helbling - You taught me that there's power in vulnerability. Keep doing what you're doing! The world needs your message.

Rye D'orazio - For teaching me that EROI (eternal ROI) is more important than anything.

Tom Skoulis - for always being a source of wisdom and keeping me centered on what's most important. I love our lunches and hope they continue!

Built to Lead - Chet Scott, David Deck and Rachel Hanson - the work you all are doing is life-transforming. I can't thank you enough for building into me.

Scott Dinsmore - We lost you too soon but our work together was such an inspiration for me and no doubt a part of this book-writing process.

Studio 8e8, especially Josh Scott, Josh Moore and Joel Hafner - Thanks guys for helping me bring some of my thoughts and ideas to life through videos and podcasts.

The River Radio, especially Dave Stephens - It's been a privilege to partner with you and big thanks for lending me your studio to record the audio book.

Dave Samuel - Thanks for bringing the book to life on audio. You're so talented.

Denae Hively and Nicole Bryant - You both rock and are a big part of this message and helping people.

Dr. Russell Barkley - I had no idea our interview on ADHD would bring me to your talk about Intention Deficit Disorder - it was perfect timing. Thank you for being so willing to talk to me.

Jeff Fromm - Thank you for your encouragement and support during this process.

Eric Nichols - Thank you for your friendship and encouragement. I love your focus on always getting better and learning. Bowling Green soccer is in great hands.

AJ Harper, Amy Port, Jen Singer and Laura Stone - You all have inspired me and played a part in some way to bring this book to fruition. I hope to work together in a deeper way in the future!

Pat Samanich - I love our talks - they are a part of this book and the journey to serve the world in a bigger way. You're next - can't wait to see "Finish" come alive!

I'm sure there are some I forgot. I apologize if that's the case. Every friend and person I interact with, I feel like I learn something from. I believe I'm a student first and learning about myself through the years, especially my failures, has been the impetus to me trying to figure out what's worked and what hasn't. It's a never-ending process. Living with intention isn't always easy. I'm definitely not perfect at it but the awareness of it and the daily attempt to be more intentional will always be a driving force.

Finally, I want to acknowledge you, the reader, once again for your support and investing the time to build yourself so you can build into others.

NOTES

1 Whatshakin3, "Dr Russell Barkley ADHD Intention Deficit Disorder." June 2, 2014. YouTube video. https://www.youtube.com/watch?v=JowPOqRmxNs.

2 "New Study Reveals Just How Many Thoughts We Have Each Day." *Newshub*. July 20, 2020. https://www.newshub.co.nz/home/lifestyle/2020/07/new-study-reveals-just-how-many-thoughts-we-have-each-day.html.

3 Csikszentmihalyi, Mihaly. *Flow: The Psychology of Optimal Experience.* New York: Harper Perennial Modern Classics, 1991.

4 "Mental Health By the Numbers." National Alliance on Mental Health. https://www.nami.org/mhstats. Accessed September 16, 2022.

5 "COVID-19 pandemic triggers 25% increase in prevalence of anxiety and depression worldwide." World Health Organization. March 2, 2022. https://www.who.int/news/item/02-03-2022-covid-19-pandemic-triggers-25-increase-in-prevalence-of-anxiety-and-depression-worldwide.

6 "2020 USA General Statistics." Save.org. https://save.org/about-suicide/suicide-statistics/. Accessed September 16, 2022.

7   Eurich, Tasha. *Insight: Why We're Not as Self- Aware as We Think, and How Seeing Ourselves Clearly Helps Us Succeed at Work and in Life.* Crown Business, 2017.

8   Collins, Jim. "The Stockdale Paradox." *JimCollins.com.* https://www.jimcollins.com/concepts/Stockdale-Concept.html.

9   Clear, James. *Atomic Habits: Tiny Changes, Remarkable Results: An Easy & Proven Way to Build Good Habits & Break Bad Ones.* New York, NY: Avery, an imprint of Penguin Random House, 2018.

10 NFL Season, "Reggie Bush Pulls Up On Drew Brees DOING WHAT IT TAKES TO BE GREAT, GRINDS LONG AFTER PRACTICE." 16 December 2019. YouTube video. https://www.youtube.com/watch?v=P7OUhs86sdQ&feature=youtu.be.

11 Duckworth, Angela. *Grit: The Power of Passion and Perseverance.* New York: Scribner, 2018.

12 Slater, Daniel. "Elements of Amazon's Day 1 Culture." AWS Executive Insights, 2001. https://aws.amazon.com/executive-insights/content/how-amazon-defines-and-operationalizes-a-day-1-culture/.

13 Covey, Stephen R. *The 7 Habits of Highly Effective People: Restoring the Character Ethic.* Thorndike, Me.: G.K. Hall, 1997.

14 Marshall, Frank, David Koepp, and George Lucas. *Indiana Jones and the Kingdom of the Crystal Skull.* United States: Paramount Pictures Corporation, 2008.

15 Piper, John. *Desiring God: Meditations of a Christian Hedonist.* New York: Multnomah Books, 1996.

ABOUT THE AUTHOR

Jon Giganti is a vice president at CCC Intelligent Solutions, a multibillion-dollar software-as-a-service (SaaS) company. He's also a keynote speaker who helps organizations, teams, and individuals score sustainable wins. Jon resides in New Albany, Ohio, with his wife, Michelle, and three children. Connect at JonGiganti.com

JON GIGANTI WILL HELP YOU LIVE WITH INTENTION.

Follow him on all of your favorite social media platforms today.

WITH INTENTION PODCAST

LISTEN AT
JONGIGANTI.COM

WITH INTENTION COURSE

Find your path to uncommon results, unleased influence, and ultimate fulfillment today.

VISIT JONGIGANTI.COM

BLOCKCHAIN
VERIFIED IP™

Powered by Easy IP™